H. TOLLEY and K. ORRELL

Yorkshire
and North Linc

THIRD EDITION

CONTENTS

The new Local Government Areas *p. 2*
1 The Pennines *p. 3*
2 The Vale of York *p. 19*
3 East Yorkshire *p. 26*
4 The Yorkshire Coast *p. 33*
5 Humberside *p. 40*
6 Scunthorpe and North Lincolnshire *p. 49*
7 Teesside *p. 57*
8 The Yorkshire Coalfield *p. 65*
9 Sheffield and the Don Valley *p. 74*
10 The West Yorkshire Conurbation *p. 84*
   Acknowledgements *p. 97*

GEOGRAPHY OF THE BRITISH ISLES SERIES
GENERAL EDITOR: A. V. HARDY

CAMBRIDGE UNIVERSITY PRESS
CAMBRIDGE
LONDON NEW YORK NEW ROCHELLE
MELBOURNE SYDNEY

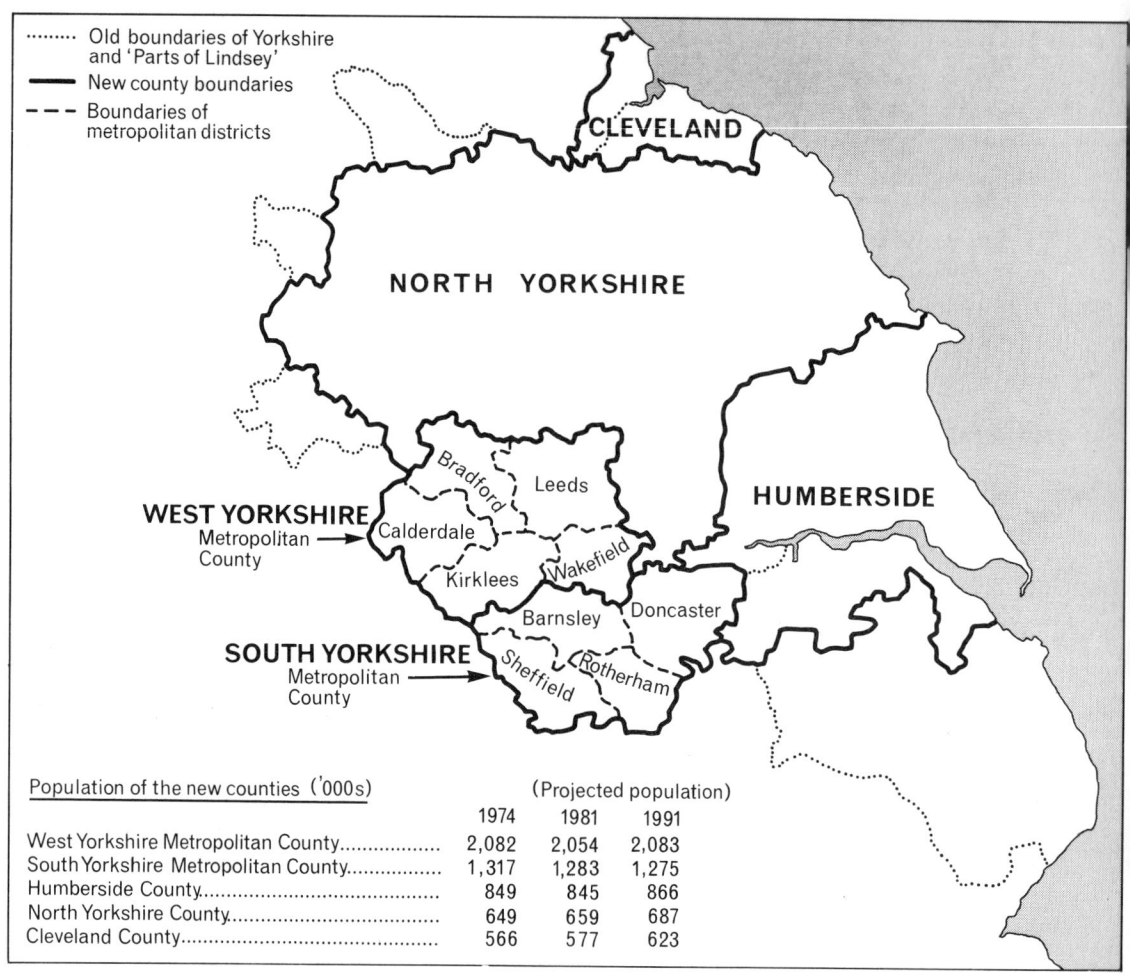

The new Local Government Areas

In April 1974 local government re-organisation affected many of the old counties of England, like Yorkshire and Lincolnshire as well as most urban and rural districts. Some counties were first established in medieval times and their boundaries had become inconvenient for modern purposes. As towns grew they spread across local government boundaries so that in many places one 'town' was being run by several local councils. Today local government provides many more services than in the past and these can be run most efficiently if the population of an area is reasonably large. Under the re-organisation of local government of April 1974, the number of areas has been reduced to give larger units more suited to modern needs.

The map on this page shows that Yorkshire and Lincolnshire have been divided into five counties each of which is subdivided into districts. These districts are larger and fewer in number than the old urban and rural districts which they have replaced.

In this book, the term 'Yorkshire' is used to include the new metropolitan counties of West and South Yorkshire, the counties of North Yorkshire and Humberside, and the southern part of Cleveland county. The names of the new counties and county districts are given where appropriate. In chapter 6, the term 'North Lincolnshire' is used to describe that part of the new county of Lincolnshire north of a line from Lincoln to Skegness.

1 | THE PENNINES

1   *Scar House and Angram Reservoirs*

The photograph in Fig 1 was taken from the air looking down on the valley of the River Nidd near its source on the slopes of Great Whernside (704 metres or 2,310 feet), a peak in the Yorkshire Pennines. Notice the heather and grass covered moors on the upper slopes and the walled fields of rough pasture on the valley sides. There are no trees to be seen and the only house which is clearly visible stands towards the bottom right, near to the dam wall.

The Pennine Hills are often called the 'Backbone of England' because they form a long chain of uplands stretching from Northumberland to the English Midlands. In Yorkshire they consist of rolling plateau country broken by occasional higher peaks and the deep valleys of the east and south-east flowing rivers, known as dales. They divide counties which face towards the North Sea from those which look out over the Irish Sea. A map will show that in many places local government boundaries follow the Pennine crest. In others they run further west to take in the western slopes and part of the 'Forest' of Bowland, and Ribblesdale. Notice that the Pennines make up the western third of the area described in this book and the Vale of York the middle third. The eastern third consists of various uplands and lowlands lying between the estuary of the River Tees and the south bank of the Humber estuary.

Water supplies from the Millstone Grit Moors
The two areas of water in the picture are the Angram and Scar House Reservoirs. Notice how they are fed by streams flowing off the surrounding moorland. They help to provide Bradford, forty-eight kilometres (thirty miles) to the south, with its water supply. The two dam walls hold back millions of litres of water. They are built of the local Millstone Grit which was quarried from a nearby hillside. This rock is non-porous so that many surface streams of pure water, fed

by the heavy Pennine rainfall, flow across it to fill the reservoirs. In the past, the same rock was used because of its hard and gritty nature to make mill stones. The dry stone walls which divide the lower slopes of the valley into fields are also built of it. Some of the walls run into the water. When the reservoirs were built, a little farmland was flooded and the few people who lived in this bleak upland valley had to move to new homes.

Many Yorkshire towns receive their water from reservoirs on the Millstone Grit moors. Sheffield has a large number on tributaries of the River Don and can also draw water from reservoirs on the River Derwent in Derbyshire. Leeds Corporation Waterworks serve more than 600,000 people in Leeds and surrounding areas. The amount of water available each day is over 164 million litres (36 million gallons) which comes from the following sources:

i. From Pennine Reservoirs
    (a) The Washburn Valley Reservoirs   91 million litres (20 million gallons)
    (b) The Ure Valley Reservoirs   41 million litres (9 million gallons)
ii. From the Yorkshire River Derwent   32 million litres (7 million gallons)

                                 164 million litres (36 million gallons)

Fig 2 shows how the water reaches Leeds. Notice that the coalfield area, which is densely peopled and has polluted rivers, has no important reservoirs. The lands to the east are too low for the gravity feed of water and are valuable farmland. The limestone areas in the north west are high, thinly populated, and have a heavy rainfall. However, limestone is permeable and has few surface streams; it is soluble in rainwater too, making it hard. Hard water needs more soap to make a lather and leaves deposits of calcium carbonate inside kettles and pipes. For these reasons the main reservoirs shown on the figure are all on Millstone Grit.

The geology map (Fig 3) and the sections (Fig 4) show the Carboniferous Limestone outcrops in the north west in the heart of the Pennines. It is almost the oldest rock found in the region; since it was laid down 350 million years

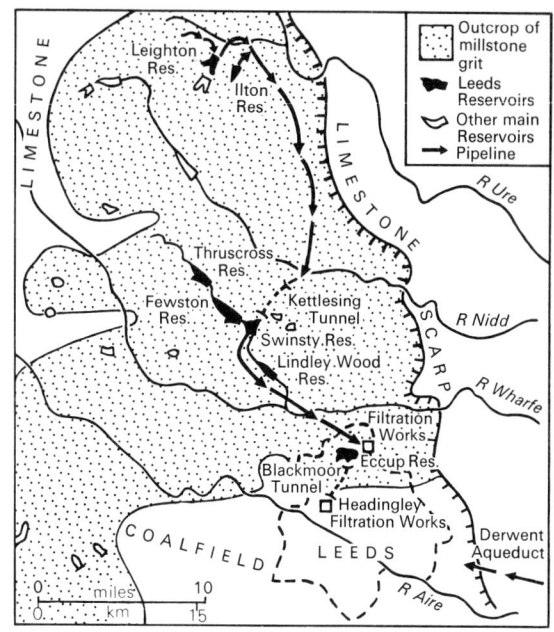

2 *Leeds Corporation Waterworks*

ago, it has been covered by younger rocks which are shown above it in the key.

Section *A–B* shows that in the south the rocks have been folded into an anticline with its crest along Yorkshire's western boundary. In section *C–D* notice that the rocks have been fractured along faults in the west and then tilted down to the east. This northern area of the Pennines is known as the Askrigg Block. Throughout Yorkshire and North Lincolnshire the rocks dip eastwards. In the higher west, the younger rocks have been eroded away so that in many places there are outcrops of Carboniferous Limestone. To the west of Leeds and Sheffield, a Millstone Grit cap forms the heather-covered moors which separate the Yorkshire and Lancashire coalfields. Notice that in the east, there are lowland vales cut in soft clay, and escarpments of more resilient rocks.

The Malham District

Forty-eight kilometres (thirty miles) north west of Leeds in the Yorkshire Dales National Park, and near the source of the River Aire, is the village of Malham. The block diagram (Fig 5) shows the area around the village, as seen from the south west. The sides are cut away to show the geology of the district. Because of its interest-

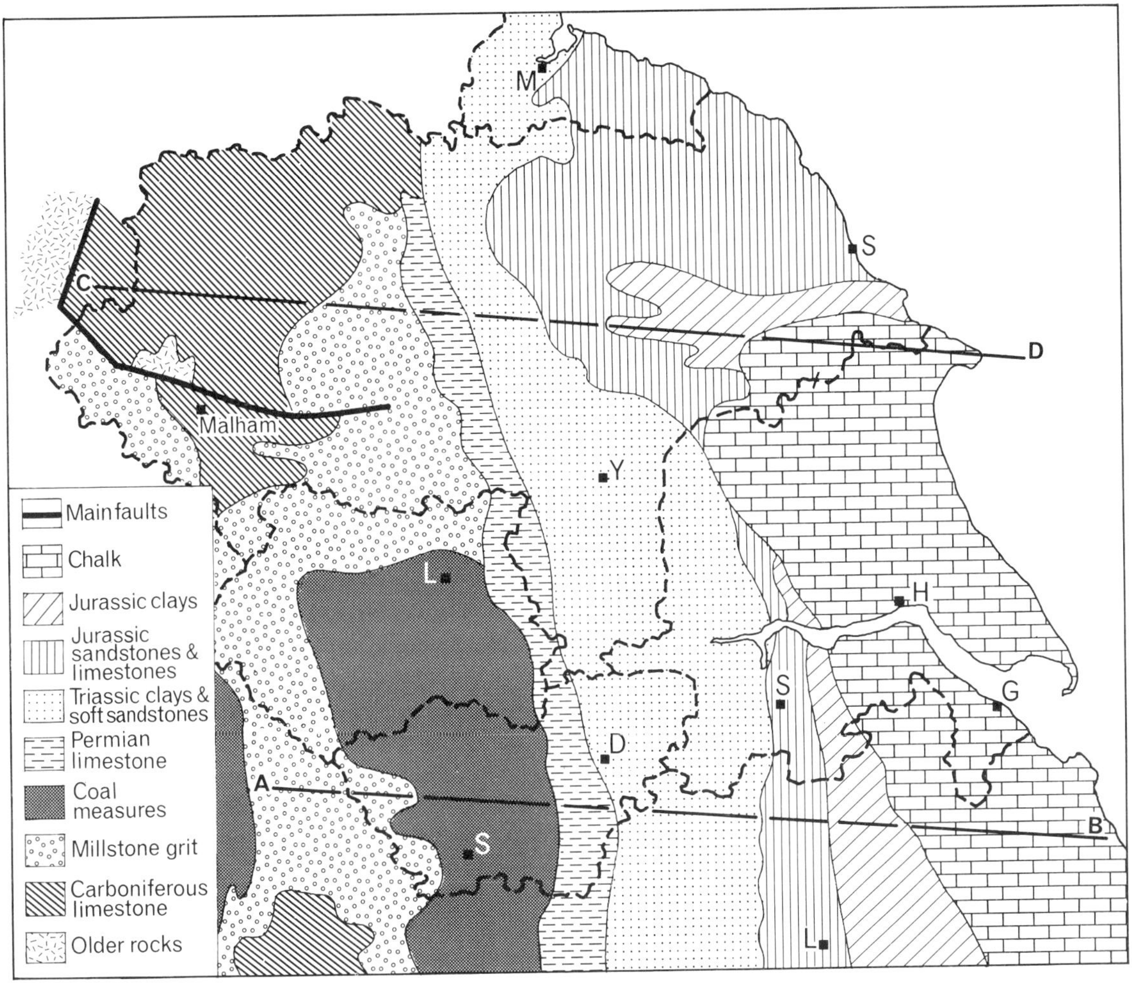

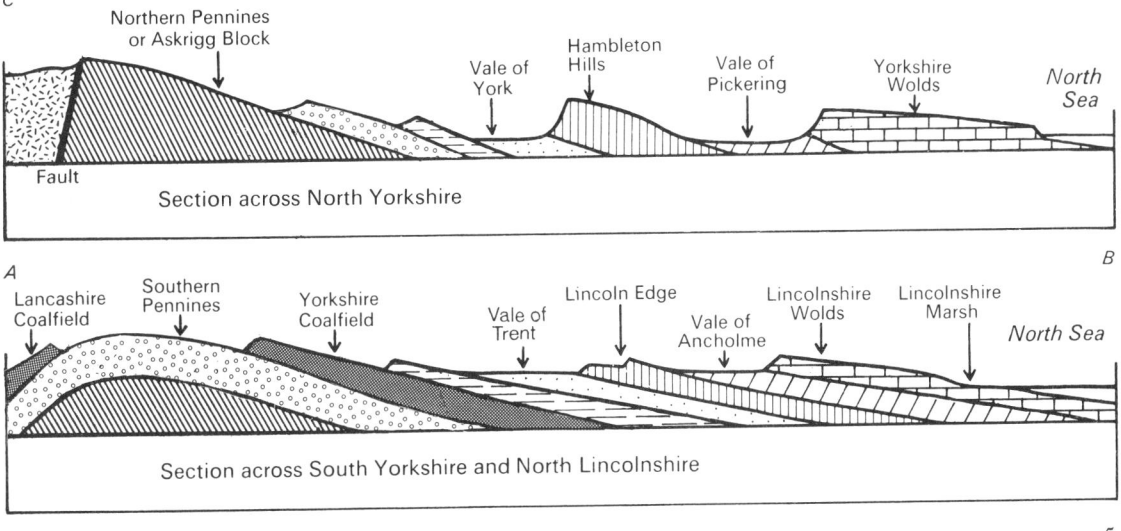

3 *The Geology of Yorkshire and North Lincolnshire*

4 *Geology sections across Yorkshire and North Lincolnshire (see Fig 3 for key to shading)*

ing limestone or 'karst' scenery the area is visited by thousands of students and tourists each year. Many of them walk along the route marked on the diagram.

From the village the route runs along the lower slopes of Cawden, a hill of coral limestone. When this area was a warm sea in Carboniferous times, the hill was a coral reef. Such hills, and there are several in the Malham district, are called reef knolls. Beyond Cawden, to the north, can be seen a steep escarpment of limestone rising 120 metres (400 feet) to over 360 metres (1,200 feet) above sea level. The diagram shows that it follows the line of the Middle Craven Fault. Uplift along the northern side of the fault brought the limestone to the surface, but to the south it is buried beneath younger rocks, the Bowland Shales.

To climb the escarpment the route leaves the road at Gordale House and follows the valley of Gordale Beck, a deep narrow gorge, shown in the photograph (Fig 6). Notice the layers or beds of limestone forming vertical cliffs or 'scars'; these are so common in the Pennines that the limestone is often called the Great Scar Limestone. The lower slopes are less steep and are formed of fragments of rock weathered from the scars. Such slopes are called screes. The flat floor of the valley consists of partly rounded boulders and gravel washed down by the beck in times of flood. The wall in the foreground is built of them.

In Gordale the beck plunges over two waterfalls and at one point passes under a natural limestone arch. This gives a clue to how the gorge was formed. Many thousands of years ago, the beck probably flowed underground through a series of caverns and passages as shown in Fig 7. Rising in Great Close Mire on impervious rocks, it flowed at the surface until it reached the limestone. Because of its many joints or cracks, this rock allowed the water to seep underground. As limestone is soluble, the joints were gradually widened to form caverns linked by narrower passages. Stalactites and stalagmites would grow down from the roof and up from the floor as lime-rich water dripped from the cavern walls and partly evaporated.

At the foot of the escarpment the stream must have re-appeared from a cave as a spring. As the caverns were enlarged their roofs finally collapsed to form a gorge, leaving behind only the limestone arch. Even today, much of the water finds its way underground as is shown by the many springs at the foot of the gorge. There are many cave systems still in existence in the Yorkshire Pennines which are popular with potholers from all over the north. One of the most famous is Gaping Gill Hole on the slopes of Ingleborough. Its main chamber is

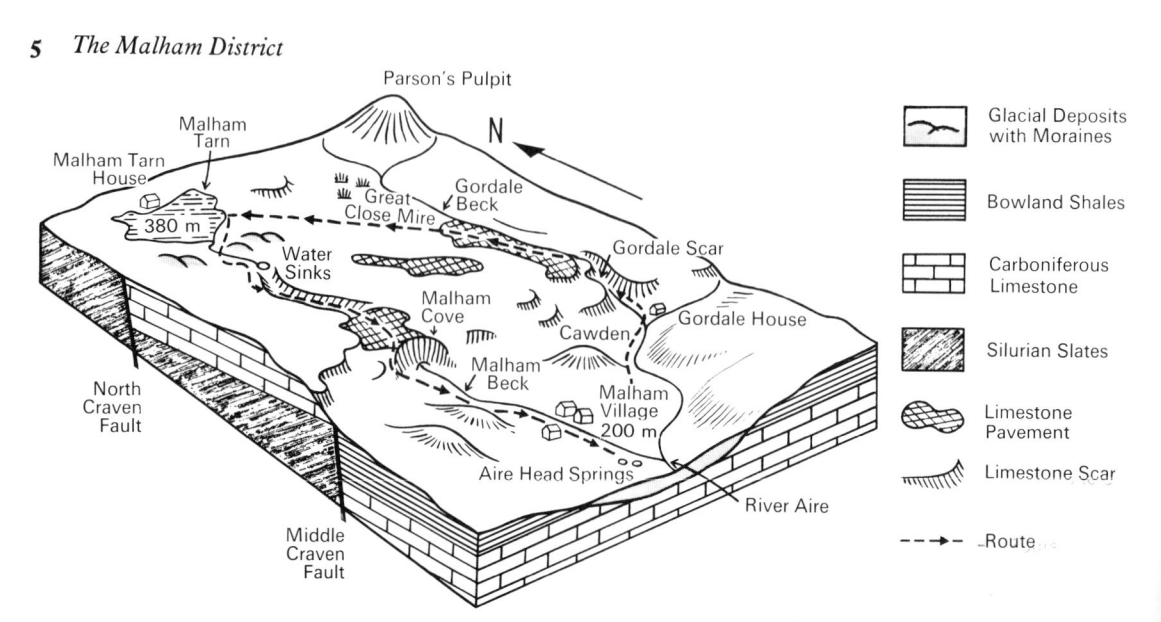

5 The Malham District

104 metres (340 feet) below the surface, 152 metres (500 feet) long, 27 metres (90 feet) wide and 34 metres (110 feet) high.

From the top of Gordale Scar, the route runs north west to Malham Tarn (Fig 5). At first it crosses bare outcrops of limestone and the short, green grass which the thin limy soils support. Nearer the Tarn, impervious slates, partly covered by glacial deposits, have been brought to the surface along the North Craven Fault. On their wetter more acid soils grow coarse grasses, rushes and heather. Malham Tarn lies on these impervious Silurian Slates and is dammed up by a ridge or moraine of glacial deposits across its southern end.

The stream which leaves the Tarn flows southwards until at Water Sinks it seeps underground at a sink or swallow hole. From here a dry valley leads to Malham Cove. At the end of the Ice Age, when there was much water from melting snows, the stream flowed along this valley to the Cove. There it plunged over a 100 metre (300 foot) high cliff as a huge waterfall hollowing out the rock so that it now overhangs many metres. The limestone pavement in the foreground of the photograph (Fig 8) has been formed by rainwater widening the joints in the rock. The cracks are known as grykes and the limestone blocks as clints.

At the foot of the cove (Fig 5) is the source of Malham Beck where water seeps from the base of the cliff. However, this is not the water which disappeared at Water Sinks. The latter reappears at Aire Head Springs south of Malham Village. The water in Malham Beck comes from another underground stream and the two cave systems must cross somewhere beneath the limestone plateau.

Living and Working in the Pennines
Fig 10 is a picture of Upper Wharfedale with the village of Buckden in the centre. The Pennines are thinly populated and the people live mostly in the villages and farms which nestle in the valleys. Life in this part of Wharfedale is typical of much of the Pennines.

6 *The Valley of Gordale Beck*

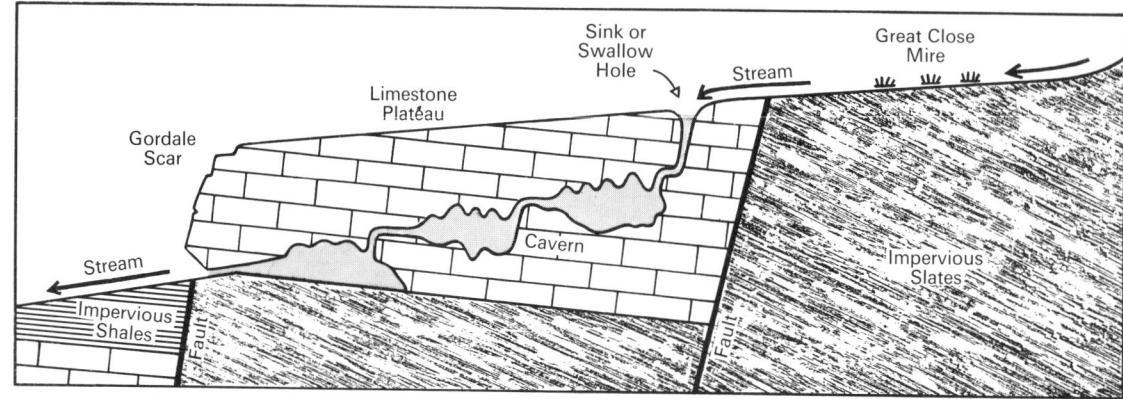

7 *Gordale Beck as it might have been before the collapse of the caverns*

The physical features of the Dale are shown in Fig 9. Many factors have helped to shape the valley: rocks of different hardnesses, the work of the Wharfe glacier during the Ice Age and the river. The Wharfe now meanders over the floor of the Dale, shifting its channel as it undercuts its banks. In this way, and by building up layers of alluvium in times of flood, the river is flattening the valley floor. In the picture (Fig 10), old river channels can be seen in some of the fields.

Buckden stands on a low mound at the mouth of a tributary valley which can be seen on the far side of the Dale in the photograph. Here, Buckden Beck has brought down sands and gravels which form a fan shaped mound sticking out across the floor of the Dale.

The map (Fig 11) is part of the 1 : 10,560 or 6 inches to 1 mile Ordnance Survey map of the Buckden area. Many features on Fig 10 can be picked out from it. The contours mark the fan or mound on which Buckden stands above the floodable valley floor. The beck provides the village with its water supply. The village, which contains several farms, is also near the best farmland along the lower slopes. The map shows that many buildings run north-west to south-east so that their main windows face south-west to get most sunshine. Slope, shelter, dry sites, water supply and nearness to farm-

8 *Limestone pavements above Malham Cove*

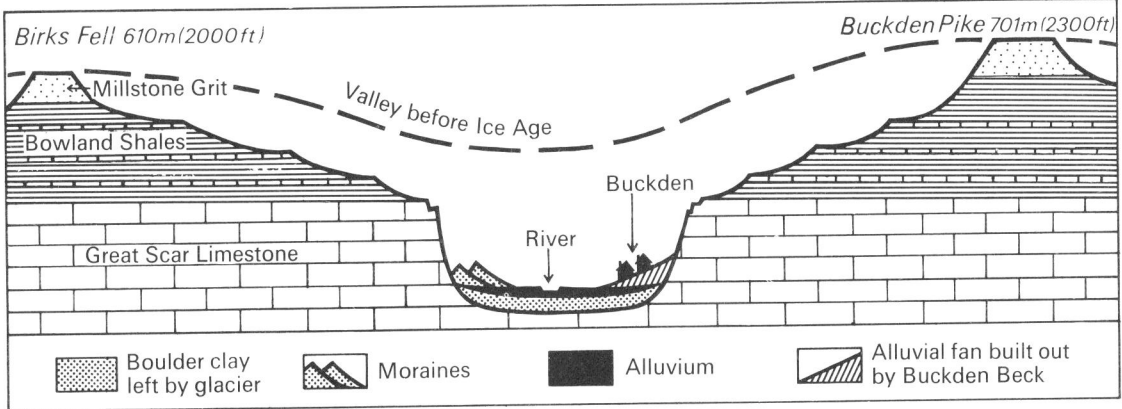

9 *A section across Wharfedale near Buckden*

land have affected the positions of most Pennine villages.

The sites were chosen by settlers who came to Yorkshire from across the North Sea. First came Saxon immigrants from the east who reached the Pennines in the seventh and eighth centuries. Later came Danes and finally Norsemen. Where these different peoples settled can often be discovered by studying place-names.

They began clearing the forested valleys where they planted crops and gathered hay. The land was divided into strips, each villager having several. Notice south of Buckden the long thin fields which are the walled-in strips of earlier days. Some fields have barns or laithes which were built for storing hay and keeping cattle in winter. Next to the farmhouses small irregular-shaped fields were built for livestock. Above the croplands, the fells were held in common and used for grazing. In the eighteenth and nineteenth centuries, some were enclosed into large rectangular fields by miles of dry stone walls but much remains as common grazing land even today. Notice on the map the large fields on the east side and the unenclosed fell north of Buckden Beck.

Pennine villages no longer need to grow all their own food. Now the farmers concentrate on rearing livestock. They sell milk, wool and lambs and young cattle for meat, or for fattening by lowland farmers. The valley floors are used for growing hay and pasturing cattle and the rough grazing on the fells for sheep flocks.

Apart from farming there are few other ways of earning a living. Lead mining was once important in some parts. Lead was worked by the Romans and during the nineteenth century it was an important industry especially in Swaledale and Arkengarthdale. There was a lead mine at the head of Buckden Beck, and Kettlewell and Grassington in Wharfedale were mining villages. The mines are now closed but fluorspar, used in steel making, is still worked from old tips of mine waste.

Limestone and Millstone Grit have always been quarried for building stone. Grindstones for knife grinding were once made in quarries west of Sheffield, while limestone was fired in kilns to make agricultural lime. Limestone is still 'burnt' today, some of the largest quarries being at Horton in Ribblesdale. Those at Wensley send limestone to Teesside steelworks.

In the last hundred years many young people have left the Pennines for more attractive jobs in the towns. Buckden school is now closed. The few children living in the village go to the primary school at Kettlewell or the secondary school at Grassington. Railways like the single track to Hawes in Wensleydale have closed through lack of passengers and trade as well as through competition from the motor car.

Cars now bring people to the Pennines for holidays or day trips. Old cottages have been converted into holiday homes while caravans and tents are familiar sights. Buckden's two general stores, one of which is the village post office and petrol station, sell souvenirs and postcards as well as groceries. Many houses and farms have 'Bed and Breakfast' signs or sell teas and refreshments. Inns like the 'Buck Inn' cater for tourists as well as villagers and big houses have become guest houses or youth hostels. Two National Parks, one in the Yorkshire Dales, the other in the Derbyshire Peak District but including parts of south west Yorkshire, have been set up. One of their many aims is to help protect the countryside by the control of any new development.

Lowlands Farm, Askrigg in Wensleydale
Lowlands Farm is typical of many Pennine farms. The farmer keeps a herd of dairy cows in the valley and a sheep flock which spends most of its time on the fells. The photograph (Fig 12) shows the farm buildings and behind them the old market centre of Askrigg. In the background, the northern slopes of Wensleydale rise over 533 metres (1,750 feet). The main windows of the ivy-covered farmhouse look southwards towards the River Ure less than a kilometre (half a mile) away. Notice it has stone walls and a flagstone roof. To the right is the asbestos-roofed dairy and cowshed where the twenty-five milk cows, all pedigree Northern Dairy Shorthorns, are milked twice a day. Behind the cowshed is a barn for hay; the low stone building houses the two tractors. Beside the cows waiting to be milked are two pieces of hay-making machinery, one for turning and one for raking the hay. Also on the farm are two stone built laithes. These stand in the hay meadows to save the carting of hay and manure to and from the main buildings. Details of the farm are set out in the table on page 12.

The farmer sells milk, fat lambs, store cattle (bullocks) for fattening, and wool; he also sells a few of his best young rams for breeding. Until 1963 the milk went to the Express Dairies Depot at Leyburn, then to London or the West Yorkshire towns. Now it goes to the Milk Marketing Board's cheese factory at Hawes where the famous Wensleydale cheeses are made. The livestock is sold at the Hawes auction market mainly in Autumn and Winter. The wool goes to the British Wool Marketing Board's local depot for sale by auction.

The farm is shown in Fig 13. In 1921 it consisted of only 37 hectares (91 acres); since then more land has been bought or rented so that now

10 *Buckden village in Upper Wharfedale as seen from X in Fig 11*

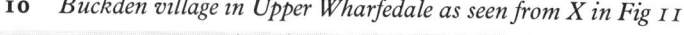

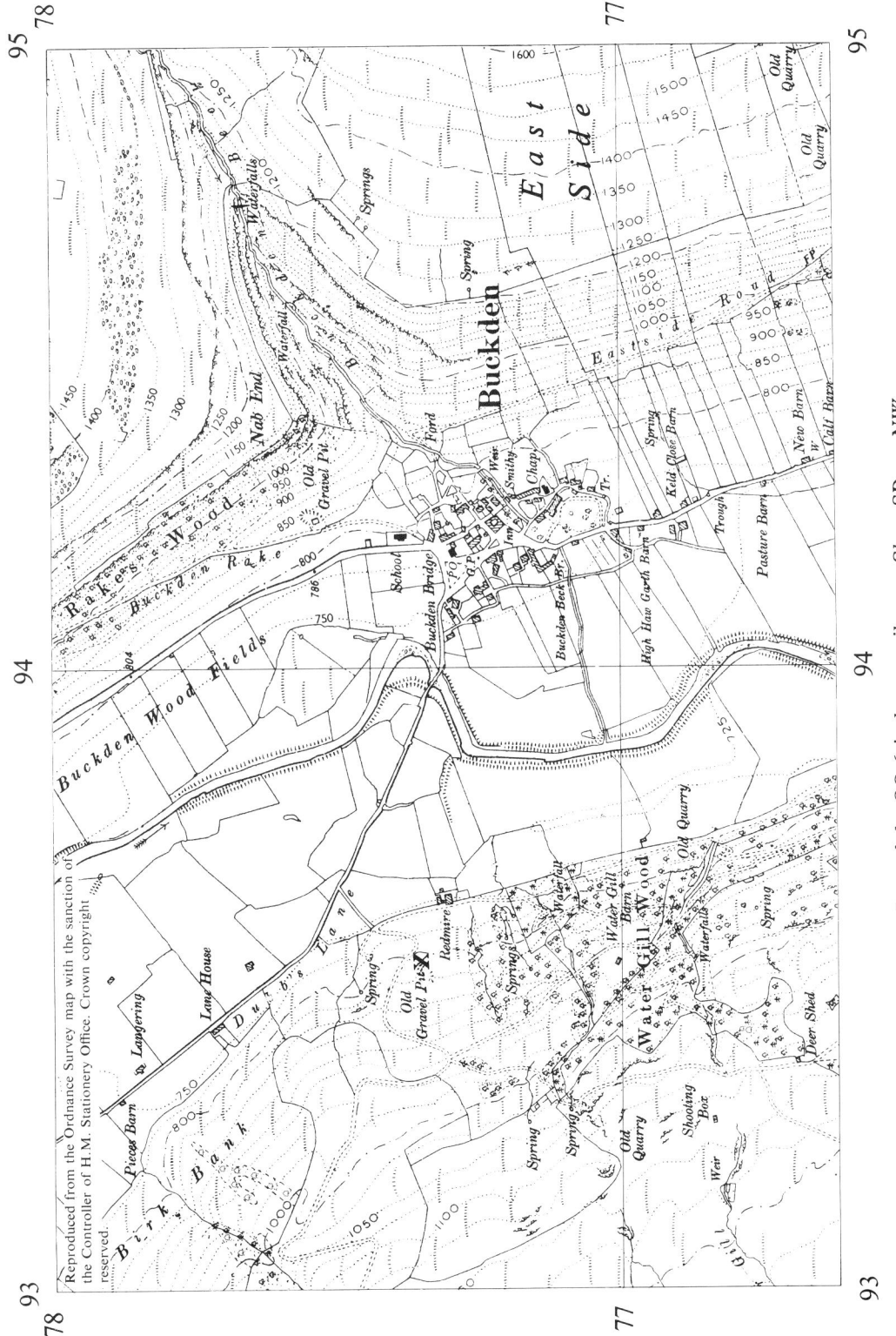

11 Part of the OS 6 inch to 1 mile map Sheet SD 97 NW

there are more than 101 hectares (250 acres). Notice that the land is either hay meadow, improved pasture or rough grazing. The climate of the Pennines is too cool, damp and cloudy for crops such as cereals, but conditions in the valleys are ideal for grass.

LOWLANDS FARM, ASKRIGG, WENSLEYDALE.
Height above sea level 207 metres (678 feet).
Size 101 hectares (250 acres).

Types of land	22 hectares (55 acres) of hay meadow
	14 hectares (35 acres) of pasture
	65 hectares (160 acres) of rough grazing
Total	101 hectares (250 acres).
Livestock	
Sheep	180 Swaledale ewes.
	200 (approx.) Lambs each year.
	3 Rams for breeding.
	Grazing rights for 120 sheep on Askrigg Common.
Cattle	25 Milk cows.
	50 Young stock. (Heifers to replace milk cows and bullocks for sale as stores).
	1 Bull.
	All Northern Dairy Shorthorns.
Poultry	20
Dogs	2 Working dogs.
Workers	Apart from the farmer himself there is 1 full time worker, the cowman, who also helps with general work. Part-time help is used for haymaking.
Farm Equipment	2 Ferguson tractors.
	3 Milking machines.
	Manure spreader.
	Artificial Fertiliser Spreader.
	General purpose trailer.
	Hay-making machinery for cutting, spreading and turning. A baler is hired when needed.

The Pennines receive more rain than any other part of the County (Fig 14). The cross section shows how the prevailing westerly winds bring much rain to the hills but far less rain to the rest of Yorkshire. Oughtershaw Hall in the Pennines is wetter at all seasons than the other three places for which graphs have been drawn. It receives more than 102 mm (4 inches) of rain in all months but May and June with a maximum in Winter. York, in the lowlands to the east of the Pennines, receives least, with a maximum in late summer.

12 *Lowlands Farm, Askrigg in Wensleydale*

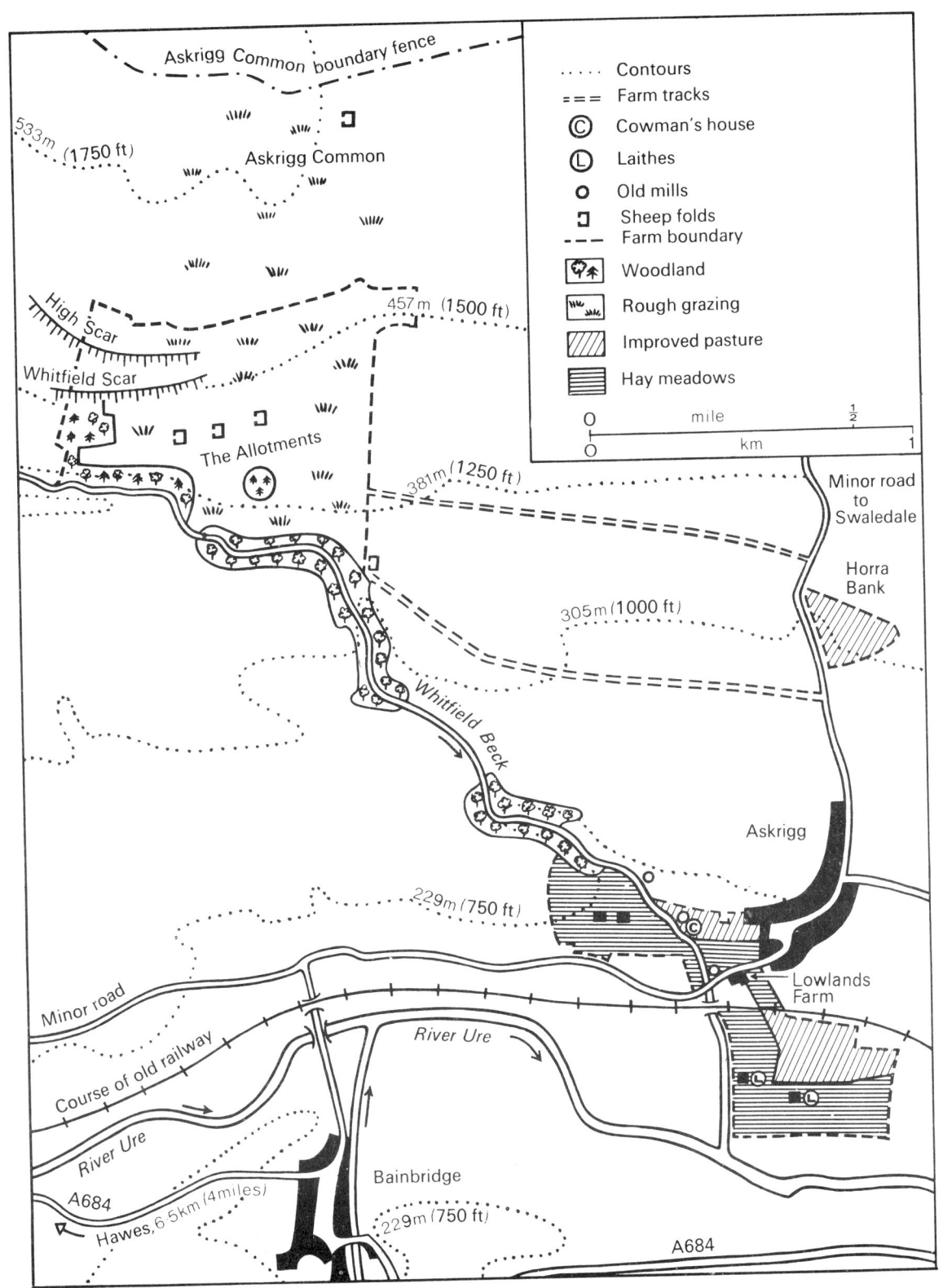

13 *A plan of Lowlands Farm*

The farmer's work throughout the year is affected by the weather. Between November and early April he keeps the cattle in the laithes, feeding them on hay and concentrates. The spring lambs which are being fattened for sale spend the winter on the rough grazings except during severe snow storms when they are brought down to the farm. If they are caught in snow drifts, the farm's two sheep dogs can smell them even through the snow. Even so, the farmer may lose many sheep in a severe winter.

In April, the ewes are brought down to Lowlands for lambing time which lasts until mid-May, while the cattle are grazed on the improved pastures. The stock are kept off the meadows until the end of June when hay making begins. The farmer hopes for a dry sunny July to dry out the hay and allow him to gather it into the barns. After haymaking, the meadows are fertilised and then grazed by the cattle until November.

The sheep and lambs spend the summer from mid-May onwards on the fells and rough grazings where the wool is clipped in late June and early July. They are 'dipped' in August and October. In October the sale of the fat lambs and old ewes begins, while in November the rams are put with the ewes in 'The Allotments' for mating.

Routes Across the Yorkshire Pennines

South of Lowlands Farm, across the River Ure, is the A684 road which runs up Wensleydale into Lancashire. Notice from the map (Fig 15) that the only other main road across the Northern Pennines follows the Stainmore Pass into Westmorland. South of the River Aire, where the Pennines are narrower and lower, many roads, railways, and even canals link Lancashire and Yorkshire. They carry heavy traffic between the large industrial towns and seaports of the two counties. Notice from the map that they follow the natural routes such as the Aire Gap and the Calder Valley. Some of the least-used links, like the Huddersfield Narrow Canal and the railway across Stainmore Pass are now closed. The amount of road traffic is increasing however. The new metropolitan counties of West Yorkshire and Greater Manchester are now linked by the Trans-Pennine Motorway (M62) which avoids the narrow settled valleys and strikes out over the moors between Huddersfield and Rochdale. At Windy Hill on the county boundary it reaches a height of 372 metres (1,220 feet). Embankments and cuttings have been designed to prevent snow drifts forming and plastic-coated wire fencing has been put up to keep sheep off the carriageways.

The photograph (Fig 16) shows a freight train approaching the Woodhead Tunnel on the Sheffield to Manchester railway, which was opened in 1845. It follows the Don Valley north westwards out of Sheffield until at Dunford Bridge it reaches its highest point of 287 metres (943 feet) and enters the five kilometre (three mile) long tunnel. Notice that the line is electrified. The powerful electric locomotives can haul freight trains quickly over the steep gradients. This is a freight-only line now and the main traffic is in coal between the Yorkshire coalfield and Lancashire.

Several routes follow the Aire Gap (Fig 15). One is the Leeds–Liverpool Canal, built between 1770 and 1816. It has more than 90 locks and climbs to over 150 metres (500 feet) above sea level. With the Aire–Calder Navigation, it links the North and Irish Seas but almost no commercial traffic uses it today. More pleasure craft pass along it each year, however, and many people are anxious to keep it open for boating and fishing. Other canals into Lancashire once followed the Calder and Colne valleys. The Huddersfield Narrow Canal, less than 2·1 metres (7 feet) wide, passed through a 4,989 metre (5,456 yard) long tunnel at Standedge.

Work to do 1. From an atlas map, trace an outline of Yorkshire and North Lincolnshire and the courses of the following rivers:—Tees, Swale, Ure, Nidd, Wharfe, Aire, Calder, Don, Trent: Shade, in brown, land over 100 metres above sea level or the nearest equivalent depending on the vertical scale used in your atlas. Name the relief areas shown in the sections in Fig 4.

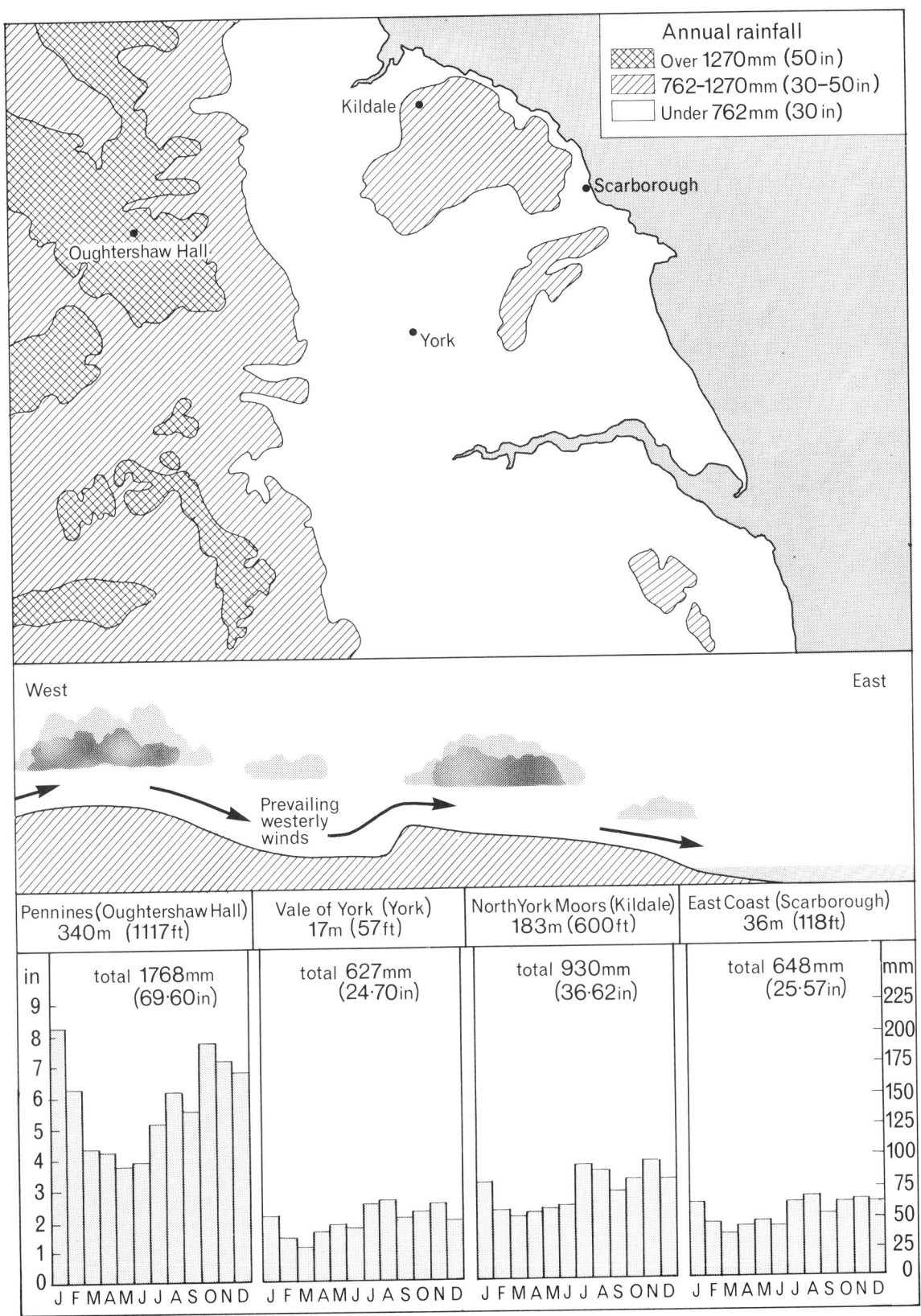

14 *A rainfall map of Yorkshire and North Lincolnshire*

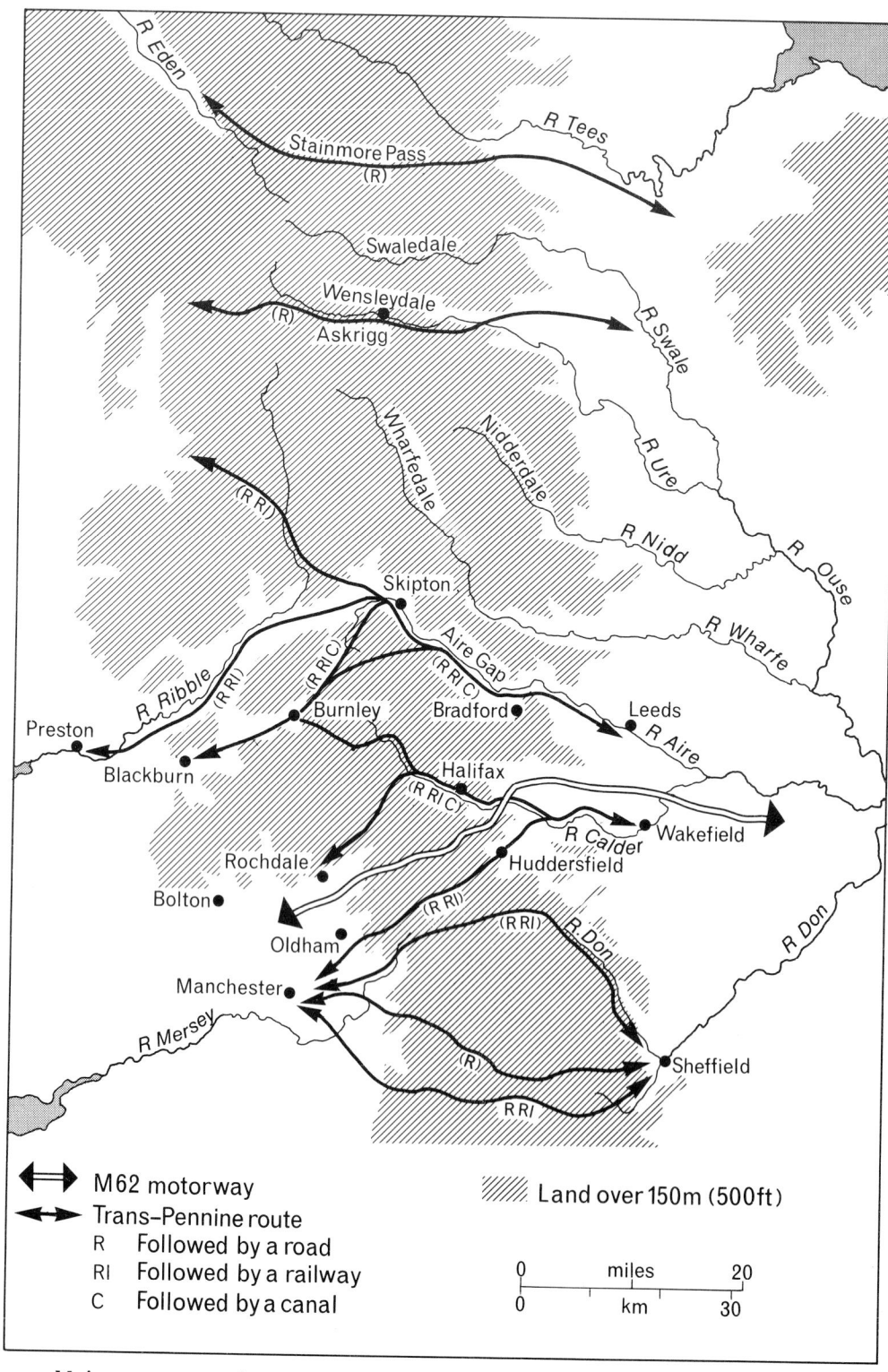

15 *Major routes across the Yorkshire Pennines*

2. Using reference books, make lists and sketches of the physical features you might find in: (a) an area composed of limestone rock; (b) a mountain valley which has been glaciated. Try to find examples of such features in the Pennines.
3. From Fig 11 draw a cross section east to west of Wharfedale along a line just beneath the word 'BUCKDEN'. Study the map and the photograph in Fig 10, then mark on your section the following: the river; the main road; the village; rough grazing land; woodland; hay meadows and pasture; springs; rock outcrops.
4. The figures given below are typical of the Yorkshire Pennines. Use them to draw a graph of temperature and rainfall. Make your graph large enough to allow you to make a table underneath showing the work at Lowlands Farm month by month. Try to make a similar table for a farm near your home.
   Kirkby Malham (395 metres or 1,296 feet). Average monthly temperatures and precipitation.

	Jan	Feb	Mar	April	May	June	July	Aug	Sept	Oct	Nov	Dec
Tem. °F	37	38	40	43	50	57	58	57	53	48	41	38
°C	2·8	3·3	4·4	6·1	10·0	13·9	14·4	13·9	11·7	8·9	5·0	3·3
Prec. in	5·6	4·4	4·9	3·5	3·4	3·5	4·7	5·8	4·2	5·7	5·6	6·1
mm	142	112	125	89	87	89	120	147	107	145	142	155

   Total: 57·5 in   1,460 mm

5. Imagine that a public meeting is being held to discuss a proposal from 'The Pennine Limestone Co. Ltd' to open a quarry just north of Buckden in Rakes Wood (see Figs 10, 11).
   (a) What arguments might the company put forward to support the proposal?
   (b) What views might the Buckden residents have?
   (c) What factors would the planning authority take into account when considering the proposal?

16 *An electrified freight train approaching Woodhead Tunnel*

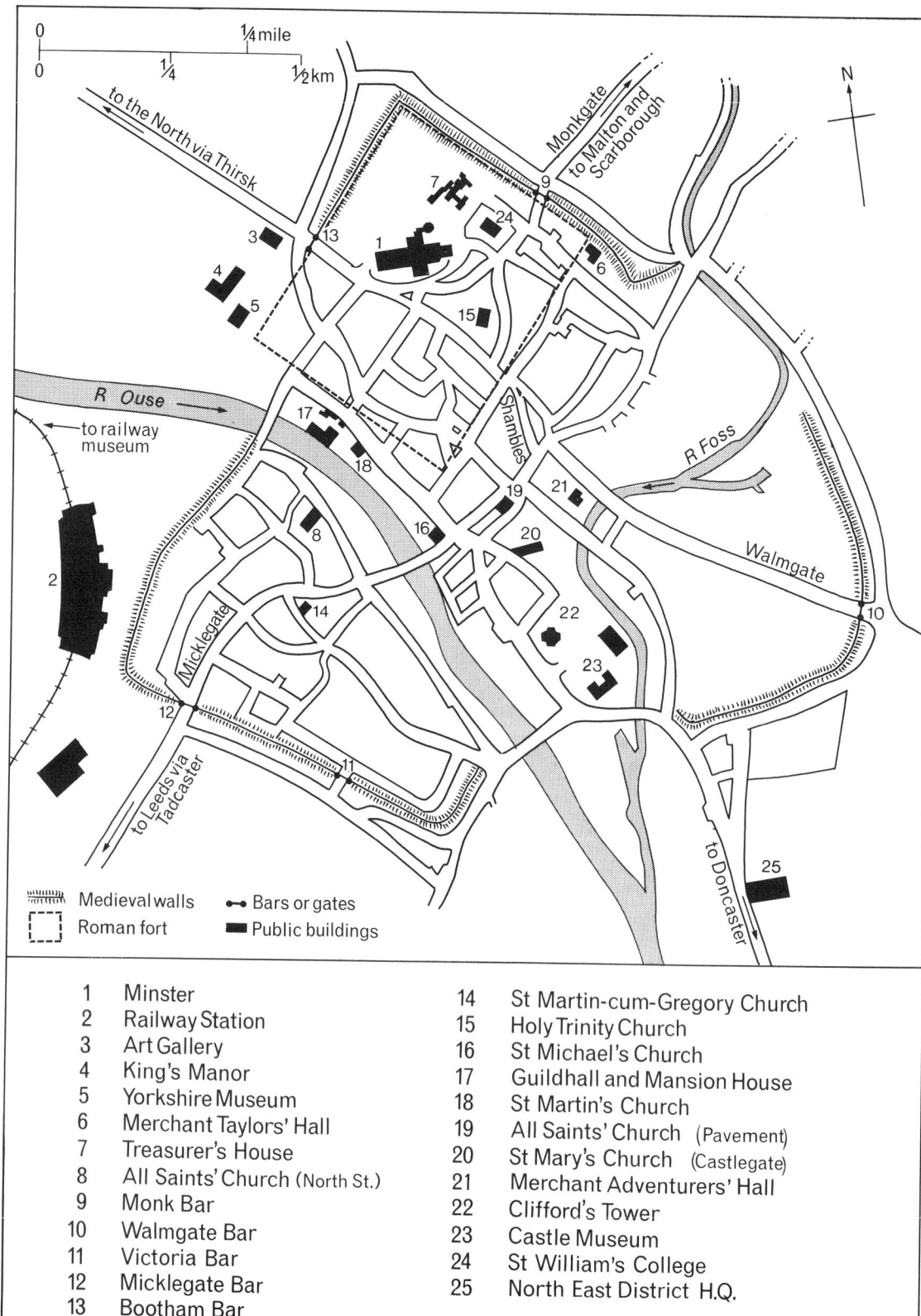

17 *The City of York*

2 | THE VALE OF YORK

18 *Monk Bar and the Minster, York*

The City of York

In A.D. 71 the Romans built a fortress in Yorkshire called 'Eboracum' which became the most important in the North of England. The street plan (Fig 17) shows that it stood to the east of the River Ouse on a site now occupied by the centre of York.

Like many Roman towns in Britain, 'Eboracum' was not only a military garrison but a civilian settlement as well. The excavation of Roman baths, houses, cemeteries and temples proves that this was situated around Micklegate on the opposite side of the river to the fort. Roman pots and coins are often discovered there when the foundations are being dug for new buildings.

An atlas map will show that 'Eboracum' was built in a commanding position in the centre of broad lowlands known as the Vale of York. This is situated between the Pennines to the west and the Yorkshire Wolds and North York Moors to the east. It merges into the Tees lowlands in the north and the Vale of Trent to the south.

The map on the following page (Map A) shows some of the reasons why the Romans chose

Map A *Based on part of OS sheet 105*

the site of York as the place to build a fort. See how thee city stands by the River Ouse; it is tidal to within one and a half kilometres (one mile) of Naburn (598455). In Roman times the tides reached even further to a point above York and small ships were able to sail up the river to the city from the North Sea. The city was built where the river has cut a gap through a narrow ridge. This ridge is part of the York moraine which runs east to west across the Vale. It consists of hummocks and mounds of sand, gravel and boulder-clay left after the melting of a glacier at the end of the Ice Age.

Before the draining of the surrounding marshes this moraine formed a natural causeway across the plain. The Romans took advantage of this and built two important roads along it. One ran south-west to Tadcaster along the route of the A64 marked on the map (see opposite page). It linked York with an important road which ran between the Roman garrisons at Doncaster and Catterick. The other ran east across the Vale of York to the Wolds. From there it followed a natural route south along the foot of the hills to a crossing point on the Humber at Brough and then to Lincoln. Other Roman roads from York ran north-east to Malton and north-west to Catterick.

The moraine gave the site at York two other advantages. The mounds of sand and gravel were well elevated above flood level and they were easily fortified, first with wood and later with stone. Fortifications like Monk Bar, shown in the photograph (Fig 18), are not Roman, but date from the twelfth and thirteenth centuries. The street plan shows that these medieval walls were built partly along the lines of the Roman fort and extended beyond the Foss to the southeast and the Ouse to the west. The defences included five gates or 'bars' which guarded the main roads into the city.

Today visitors who walk along the top of the walls obtain some excellent views over the city. Dominating the skyline are the three great towers of the Minster which can be seen beyond the gateway in the photograph. After standing for over 500 years, the Cathedral was in danger of collapse because its weight was proving too great for the soft glacial deposits on

19   The Shambles, York

which it stands. A £2 million restoration scheme was completed in 1972.

Five or six churches have previously stood on the site now occupied by the Minster. The first was built of wood as long ago as the seventh century. York is still of great importance as the centre of government of the northern province of the Church of England. Its Archbishop ranks second to the Archbishop of Canterbury in the Anglican Church.

Visitors who wander through the maze of narrow streets close to the Minster gain an impression of what York was like in the Middle Ages. In those days people were only safe when they lived within the protection of the city walls. As a result buildings were crowded together along narrow streets like the Shambles shown in the photograph (Fig 19). Here the overhanging gables are so close that in places two people can shake hands across the street through the upstairs windows.

By this time York had become the market town for the surrounding farmlands, but its real wealth was gained from the wool trade. Ships belonging to York merchants sailed down the Ouse to trade across the North Sea with ports on the continent. The craftsmen and merchants became so prosperous that they built many guildhalls and mansion houses in the city.

York ceased to be a centre for the manufacture of woollen cloth during the Industrial Revolution when its craftsmen resisted new ways of making cloth and for a time the decline in trade brought poverty to the city. Its prosperity revived later when it became a residential centre for wealthy families. Many of the old medieval streets were demolished to make way for buildings in the Georgian style.

It was in the nineteenth century that York became the centre of the network of railways shown on map A. The city is now the headquarters of the 'Eastern Region' of British Rail. Railway carriages are made and repaired in its workshops which employ nearly 3,000 people.

Today York is an important industrial city known throughout the world for chocolate and sweets made by 'Rowntree' and 'Terry'. The Rowntree factory on the northern outskirts of the city has a staff of over 7,000 people. Three kilometres (two miles) north of the city is the works of Vickers Ltd which makes microscopes and surveying instruments. Sugar beet grown in the surrounding farmlands is refined in the factory at Poppleton. With the growth of these and other industries, the population of York has increased from 17,000 in 1801 to 102,000 in 1976.

York has retained many of its ancient functions. It is still a market town for the Vale of York. A modern livestock auction mart on the eastern outskirts of the town attracts farmers and meat traders to buy and sell sheep and cattle. It has always been a military garrison and today it is the headquarters for the North East District. Its historic buildings and museums attract thousands of visitors each year. In 1963, it became a university town. The modern buildings of the university, which has about 2,500 students, are at Heslington (627503).

Modern sea-going ships are unable to sail up the Ouse today and York is no longer the important port that it was in the Middle Ages. Now the trade is carried by tugs and barges and the river forms an important inland waterway linking the city with the Humber ports.

York has maintained, though not in full, its special place in Yorkshire's local government. In the early Middle Ages the Danish kings divided Yorkshire into three Ridings or 'thridings'. Each one was represented in the 'Thing', a kind of Parliament held at York. These divisions remained until 1974, each Riding having its own County Council. York, at the junction of the three Ridings, belonged to none of them and since it had its own sheriff it was both a county and a city. In 1974 York became a district in the new county of North Yorkshire.

Farming in the Vale of York

The lowlands surrounding York are some of the richest farmlands in Britain. Their prosperity results from natural advantages combined with improvements to the land which have been made over the centuries.

The South. Today some of the best land is found around the lower course of the Ouse and to the south of the Humber. The farmworker shown in the photograph (Fig 20) is hoeing rows of tulips on a market garden near Selby. Behind him is a field of vegetables and beyond are glasshouses where lettuces, tomatoes and other crops are grown. This scene could easily be mistaken for the Fens which border the Wash. In fact, before it was drained by a Dutchman called Vermuyden in the seventeenth century, the land in the south of the Vale of York and in the neighbouring parts of north Nottinghamshire and Lincolnshire was also fenland.

The map (Fig 21) shows that the higher parts like the Isle of Axholme stood up as islands above the marsh. The Don, Idle and Torne flowed in shifting courses towards the Trent and the land was so low lying that it was often flooded at high tides. Vermuyden diverted the Idle to the south of the marsh and the Don, by way of 'Dutch River', to the north. The new courses of the rivers were built in straight lines to speed up the flow and were embanked to prevent flooding.

Despite all this, the ground was so low-lying that the soil remained waterlogged for most of the year and proved useless for arable farming. This difficulty was overcome by warping. Drains were cut from the rivers and at high tide water was led through sluice gates onto an embanked area of land. At low tide the water drained back into the rivers leaving the field covered with a layer of alluvium. This was repeated until the level of the land was built up with fertile soils called warps. Parts of Thorne Waste and Hatfield Moor, which are covered with thick layers of peat, were also reclaimed in this way. Most of the warping took place in the nineteenth century when there was an increased demand for food from the industrial towns of the West Riding. These towns are still the most important market for the farm produce of this area.

Not all of the warplands are used for market gardens. There are many farms where wheat, barley, oats, potatoes and sugar beet are grown. These are nearly all sold after harvesting and are known as cash crops. The fertile stoneless soils of the warplands favour these crops, especially potatoes. The flat relief makes it easy to use large machines and the dry sunny climate is an advantage for ripening and harvesting the cereals. Breweries like those at Tadcaster buy the best quality barley. Sugar beet is sent to the factories at York, Selby and Brigg.

Many farmers keep a dairy herd and there is some fattening of beef cattle. On such farms grass and clover are included each year in the rotation of crops. Grass crops help to maintain the fertility of the soil and provide grazing for the cattle. These in turn manure the fields, eat up sugar beet tops and graze the stubble after the cereals have been harvested. Pigs and poultry are important on some of the farms.

The map (Fig 22) shows that the warplands give way northwards to soils formed from lake-floor deposits. These were laid down during the Ice Age when ice sheets in the North Sea blocked the River Humber causing a large lake to form in the central part of the Vale of York (Fig 23). The clays and sands deposited in this lake now form a flat plain south of York at about eight metres (twenty-five feet) above sea level. In places the clays are marshy and can only be used for cattle pasture in the summer. Elsewhere they are used for cash crops like those grown on the warplands. The best of the sandy

20 *A market garden near Selby*

soils are used for market gardening and are especially favourable for carrots. In other places they are very infertile and are left as heather-covered commons.

The North. North of York the lowlands narrow and the relief is not as flat as it is in the south. Here the fields are used for pasture as well as crops and cattle, which have been reared on upland farms like the one at Askrigg in Wensleydale, are bought for fattening. In winter some of the fields are used for sheep which have been brought down from the Pennines. The main crops of the area are barley, wheat, oats, sugar beet and potatoes. Root crops such as turnips are important for feeding the livestock during the winter.

The soil map (Fig 22) shows the main reason why farming in the north differs from that further south. There are no warplands and most of the soils have been formed from boulder-clays and sands. These were left by the glacier which deposited the moraine at York. On melting it left moraines and other glacial deposits such as the boulder-clays near Ripon and Northallerton in the form of low rounded hills called drumlins. These are oval-shaped in plan and because

22 *The soils of the Vale of York*

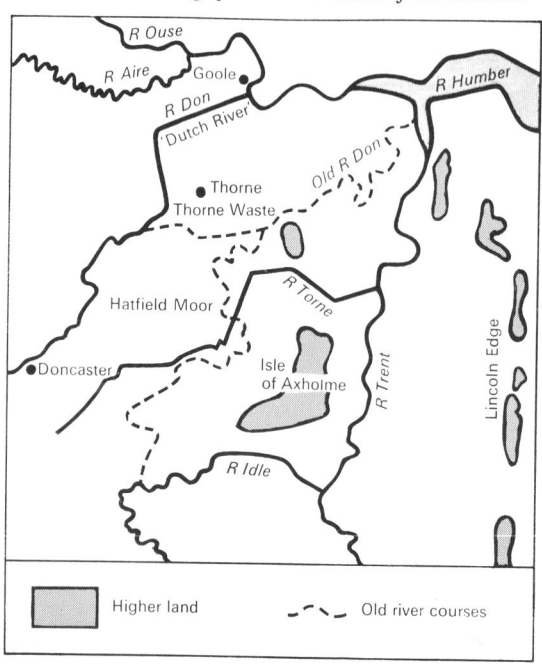

21 *The draining of the lands south of the Humber*

large numbers of them occur close together they are given the name 'basket-of-eggs-relief'.

The heavy clays are more suitable for pasture than crops and many of the hollows between the drumlins are so badly drained that they can only be used for rough grazing.

Water from the melting glacier deposited sands and gravels which are too infertile for cultivation unless they have been improved by the farmers. In some places this has been done by ploughing in clay which has been dug from beneath the sands and spread out over the fields. This process, called marling, has been used in the Netherlands to reclaim the sandy Geestlands. Over the past few years our ideas on the glaciation of the Vale of York as illustrated in the map (Fig 23) have been revised. It is now thought that the ice may have been more extensive and that the lakes, if they occurred, were much smaller. The glaciers, instead of retreating back towards their sources when the climate got warmer again, stagnated and melted from the top downwards.

24

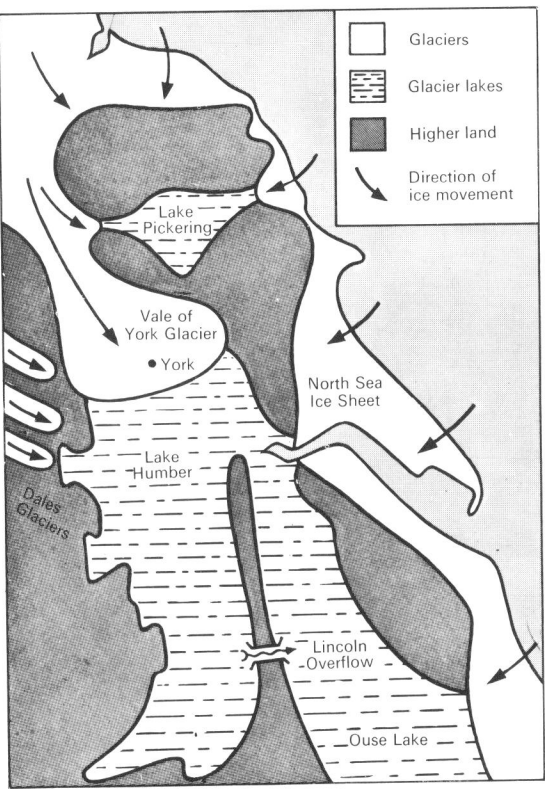

This means that features such as some glacial channels, which were once thought to have been formed by melt-water running along the edge of the glacier or by water overflowing from a glacial lake, were probably formed by water flowing in tunnels beneath the ice.

23 *Glacial Lake Humber*

Work to do
1. Find the Roman names for: Lincoln; Tadcaster; Doncaster; Catterick; Malton; Brough.
2. Make a list of the advantages of York as the site for a Roman fort.
3. Describe the modern functions of York.
4. Study the street plan (Fig 17) and make a brochure which lists the interesting things a visitor can see in York or design a poster displaying the main tourist attractions of the city.
5. Make a sketch map to show the position of York. On it mark and name: the rivers Ouse and Foss; the York moraine; the edges of the uplands to the east and west of the Vale of York; the main roads and railways converging on the city.
6. Describe the changes you would expect to see on a journey from Gainsborough to Northallerton in: (a) relief; (b) soils; (c) farming.
7. Write a paragraph describing the effects of the Ice Age on the Vale of York.
8. What natural difficulties have the farmers had to overcome to make the Vale of York more productive?

3 | EAST YORKSHIRE

24 *Harvesting barley at Westfield Farm*

Westfield Farm in the Vale of Pickering

In the photograph (Fig 24) three combines are being used to harvest a field of barley at Westfield Farm near Malton 25 kilometres (16 miles) north east of York. The harvesters cut the long stalks of barley like huge lawn mowers. The barley falls onto moving belts and is carried into the machines where the ears are stripped from the stalks. The husks are then separated from the grain which is fed into large storage bins. When these are full they are emptied into trailers through the long pipes which can be seen on the sides of the harvesters. The straw is thrown out on top of the stubble and is put into bales by the machine which is being pulled by a tractor on the right of the picture.

The baler, the tractor and two of the combines belong to an agricultural contractor from the village of Sherburn. Mr A. Milner, the owner of Westfield Farm, hires the machines at harvest time so that the crops can be gathered in as quickly as possible. Usually the work cannot start until noon because the crops are still damp from the morning dew, but it often continues until 9 p.m. Headlights are fitted on the harvesters so that work can go on after dark if necessary.

Using modern machines, two men can harvest up to ten hectares (twenty-five acres) in a day. In the past it would have taken much longer and would have needed as many as five men. This was because most of the work was done by hand. A horse-drawn machine called a reaper cut the crop and fastened it into sheaves. These were then propped up against each other, with the ears of grain at the top, to form stooks. When they were dry the sheaves were pitch-forked onto a cart and taken to the farm for threshing.

Most of the fields at Westfield Farm are large and flat like the one in the photograph. This makes it easy to use big machines like the harvester. Figure 25 shows the farm plan. The fences between some of the smaller fields have been removed, thus making it easier to use machinery.

The harvesting of cereal crops on the 83 hectare (205 acre) farm usually begins in late July. At that time of the year, Mr Milner looks anxiously at the sky hoping for the dry sunny weather which is needed for ripening and harvesting his wheat and barley. Because the farm is in the Vale of Pickering in the east of Yorkshire the likelihood of dry weather is greater than on farms in the wetter western parts of the county. This is one of the main reasons why most of the cereals in Britain are grown in the lowlands of Eastern England. A rainfall map in an atlas will show that these areas on average receive about 635 millimetres (25 in) of rain a year.

It is usually the end of August before the harvest is finished. All the cereals grown are used to feed the livestock.

The plan (Fig 25) shows that at present about half the cereals grown on the farm are wheat and the other half barley. This is to make the best use of the different soil types.

By the end of September, work on harvesting sugar beet begins. Two lorry loads a week are sent to the factory in York and some of the fields are not cleared until January. Potatoes are gathered from mid-October until mid-November and are stored in a barn until January because they fetch a good price if they are sold at that time of the year.

In 1974 Mr Milner built an intensive pig unit. All the pigs are kept inside and the sows farrow all year round. The young pigs are fed to bacon weight and then sent to a bacon factory in Thirsk. They are sent to a factory rather than to market since they are top quality bacon pigs for which the factory gives a bonus. There are 70 sows producing about 1,200 pigs a year.

There are usually about 40 beef cattle at Westfield Farm. Mr Milner buys his cattle in the spring and turns them out to grass. In the autumn they are moved into yards and fed on barley, concentrates and chopped straw. The cattle are sold in the following spring at Malton market.

Some years ago, tile drains were laid to remove wet patches from the farmland to the north of Sherburn Beck. Drainage in these fields has always been poor and at one time they were part of the marshy Sherburn Carr, which is marked on the map on the following page (Map B(a)). Like all the low-lying land on the floor of the Vale of Pickering these fields were liable to flooding by the River Derwent. The alluvium shown on the geology map (Map B(b)) was deposited by the river and the peat was formed

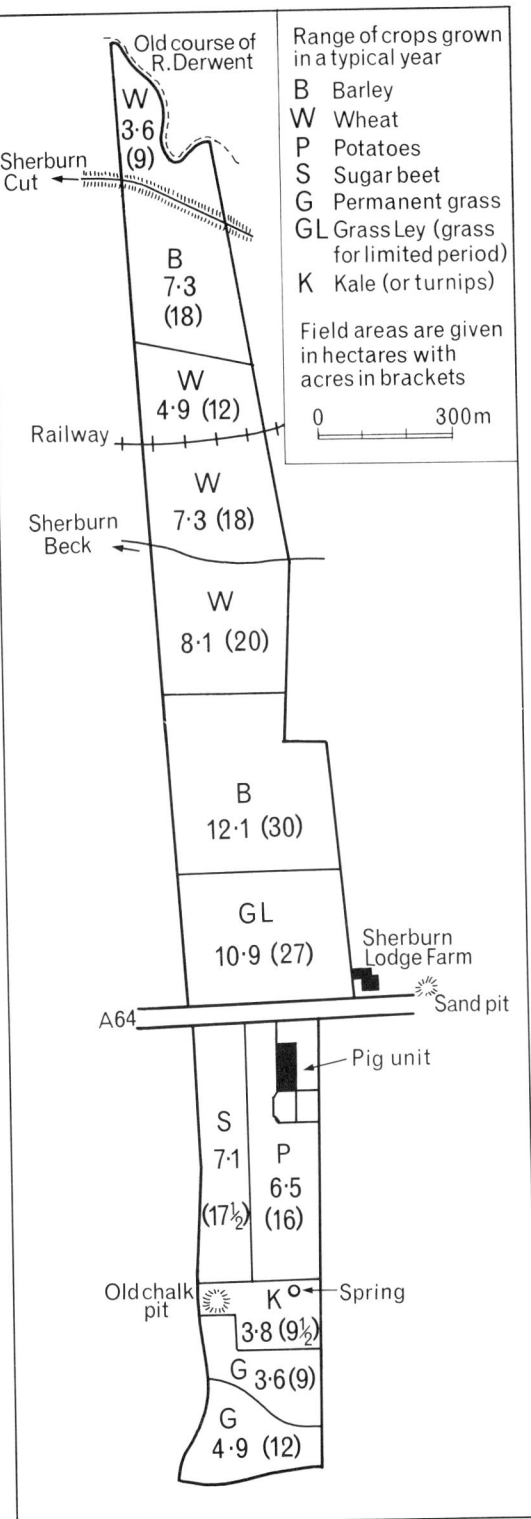

25 *A plan of Westfield Farm showing crops grown in a typical year*

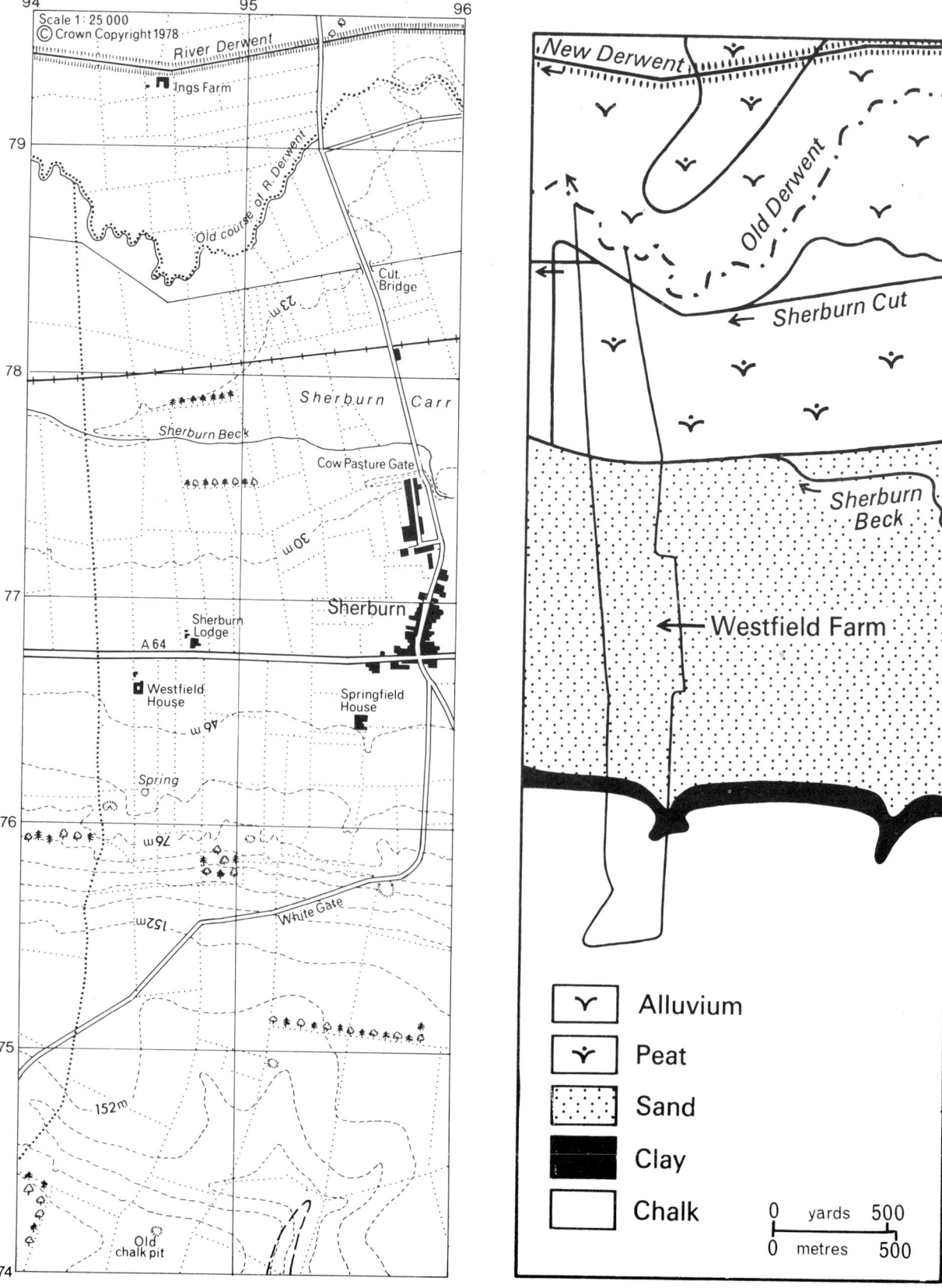

Map B (a) *Based on part of OS sheet SE 97*   (b) *The geology around Westfield Farm*

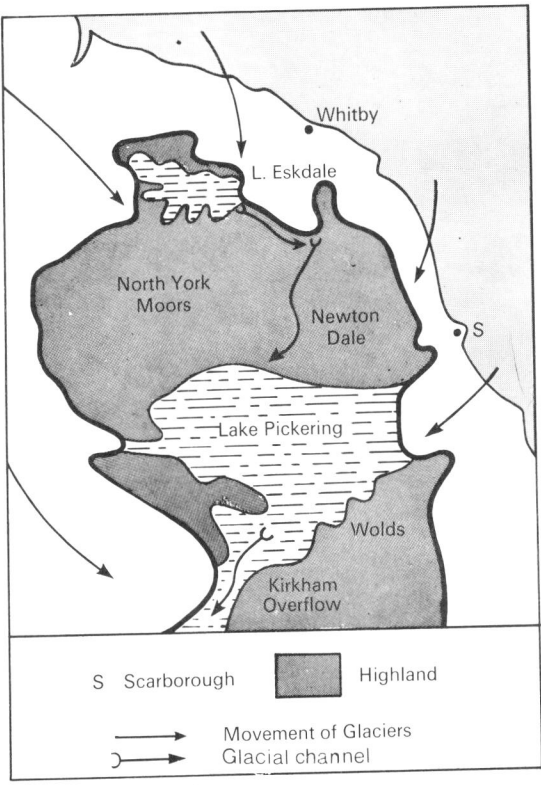

26 *Lake Pickering*

as the scarp slope of the Wolds. Along the northern edge of the Vale a similar line of villages is joined by the A170.

Lake Pickering

The recent changes that man has made in the course of the River Derwent are small compared with those which occurred in the Ice Age. Previously the river flowed east to the coast near Filey and not west to the Ouse as it does today. How the change came about is shown in the map (Fig 26). Glaciers spread on to the Yorkshire coast from the North Sea. They blocked the mouth of the River Derwent and caused Lake Pickering to form. Eventually the lake drained away when water overflowed south-west across the hills near Malton and cut Kirkham Gorge. Moraines left inland from the coast now prevent the Derwent from following its old course to the sea.

The Yorkshire Wolds

South of Westfield House (946766) the land rises steeply up the scarp of the Yorkshire Wolds. These hills reach over 250 metres (800 feet) high and form a great curve from Flamborough Head almost to the Humber. They have scarped edges to the north and west and gentler dip slopes to the south and east.

The old pit on Mr Milner's land (944761) shows that the Wolds are made of chalk. This is a porous rock and rainwater quickly sinks into the ground. Because of this there are very few streams and the drainage is mainly underground as it is in the Pennines at Malham. Springs (946761) occur where the chalk rests on a non-porous rock, like clay. There are many dry valleys where streams once flowed; a good example leaves the southern edge of the map at grid reference 953740.

Once the Wolds were used mainly for sheep rearing, but in the eighteenth century many changes began to take place. The open hills were made into fields by the planting of hedges. Then crops were sown in a new system of rotation discovered in Norfolk. Each field in turn was planted with roots, oats, clover and barley in that order. Sheep were fed on the clover in summer and on root crops like turnips in winter. The sheep in turn manured the fields.

from the remains of plants which once grew in the marsh.

Looking at Map (B(a)) you can see that drainage improvements have been made in the Vale of Pickering similar to those in the lands south of the Humber. See how a straight embanked channel has been made for the Derwent and the way in which the old meandering course of the river has been abandoned except for a small stream. Because of these improvements crops can now be grown in fields which previously were used only in the summer months as cattle pasture.

Notice also how Sherburn (959768) stands on the higher ground away from the low-lying land by the River Derwent. It is one of a line of villages which are situated above flood level at the foot of the Wolds and which are linked by the A64 road. The parish boundaries of these villages stretch from the river to the top of the Wolds' scarp. The farms are arranged in long narrow strips so that farmers like Mr Milner each have some of the flat floor of the Vale as well

Today the Wolds' farmers still rotate their crops but not in the strict order of the Norfolk system. Artificial fertilisers allow wheat, barley, potatoes and sugar beet to be grown more often than in the past and pigs and cattle are reared as well as sheep. Belts of trees like those shown on the first map on page 28 (Map B (a)) have been planted in many parts of the Wolds. These give shelter to the exposed farms, especially from easterly and northerly winds.

Holderness
The movement of glaciers marked on the map (Fig 26) brought masses of debris which were deposited as boulder-clays and sands and gravels when the ice melted. These deposits now cover the underlying rocks and form the low plain between the Wolds and the Humber known as Holderness.

When the ice left Holderness there were many swamps and even lakes, known as meres, between the ridges and mounds of the glacial deposits. Today only Hornsea Mere is left and dykes drain most of the marshes. The main river is the Hull which flows south to join the Humber. Now some of England's richest farmland is found in Holderness. In the dry climate barley and wheat flourish on its clay soils. Beef cattle are reared in the wetter areas, and pigs and poultry are fed on by-products from the seed crushing and flour mills of Hull.

North York Moors
Glacier lakes similar to Lake Pickering may have been formed in the North York Moors during the Ice Age. It has always been supposed that overflow water from the largest of these, Lake Eskdale, cut Newtondale, which is the valley shown in the photograph (Fig 27). Notice the flat top of the moors; the steep valley sides with bare outcrops of rock; the Grosmont to Pickering scenic railway on the valley floor; and absence of houses and fields. As in the Pennines, the heather and coarse grass of the moors provide rough grazing suitable only for sheep, though dairying and mixed farming are possible in some of the valleys.

Although no one has proved that Newtondale was formed in a different way it is now thought that many of the other glacial channels in the North York Moors were cut by rivers which flowed beneath the melting ice. This helps to explain why some of them run uphill in places because the streams which formed them flowed in tunnels beneath the ice under hydrostatic pressure just as water is able to run uphill in a water main. Once it was realised that many of the channels were formed in this way rather than along the edge of the ice it meant that areas which previously had been thought of as ice free were probably glaciated. Thus it seems more than likely that Lake Eskdale shown in Fig 26 (and in countless other books) never existed. Instead the valley was probably covered with a thick mass of ice which came up the dale from the North Sea to the east and over the moors from the north. When the climate began to improve it probably melted in the same way as the glaciers described on pages 24 and 25.

This part of Yorkshire is sparsely populated and the Forestry Commission have been allowed to plant trees over large areas. To preserve their natural beauty, the North York Moors have been made into a National Park. The strangest sight for visitors is on Fylingdale Moor where an Early Warning Station has been built. Here three white radomes rise up from the plateau like great golf balls. These contain the radar equipment which scans the skies for missiles as far away as Siberia.

The diagram (Fig 28) shows that the North York Moors are made of Jurassic limestones and sandstones. Notice how these dip south beneath the softer clays out of which the Derwent has carved the Vale of Pickering. The moors form a vast stretch of flat-topped plateau about 366–427 metres (1,200–1,400 feet) high. The River Esk and the tributaries of the Derwent have cut deep valleys which are called dales like those in the Pennines. Some of Yorkshire's steepest roads climb the sides of these hills especially in the north and west where they form scarp slopes.

Iron ores were once mined from the Jurassic rocks of the Cleveland Hills and used in the iron and steel works at Middlesbrough. Today cheaper and better quality ores can be imported and all the mines have been closed.

Long before drilling began in the North Sea, Whitby had its own supply of natural gas from a well in the North York Moors. Now this has

27   *Newtondale*

run dry, but a Canadian Company has found even greater supplies west of Scarborough, at Loxton and on Farndale Moor. Their drilling rig has struck enough gas to supply a town ten times the size of Whitby and the prospectors hope to find even more in the rocks beneath the moors. They have also discovered one of the world's biggest deposits of potash and I.C.I., the large chemical firm, opened a mine at Boulby on the moors near Whitby in 1973.

This employs eleven hundred men and at the moment produces 1,400 tonnes of potash a month from a depth of 1,100 metres (3,600 feet). It is hoped to continue increasing output until it reaches 1 million tonnes a year. The main use of potash is in the manufacture of fertilisers. As the mine is in a national park, much care has been taken in the design and landscaping of the site. The mine has also benefited the local people by providing more jobs in the area.

28   *A Section across East Yorkshire*

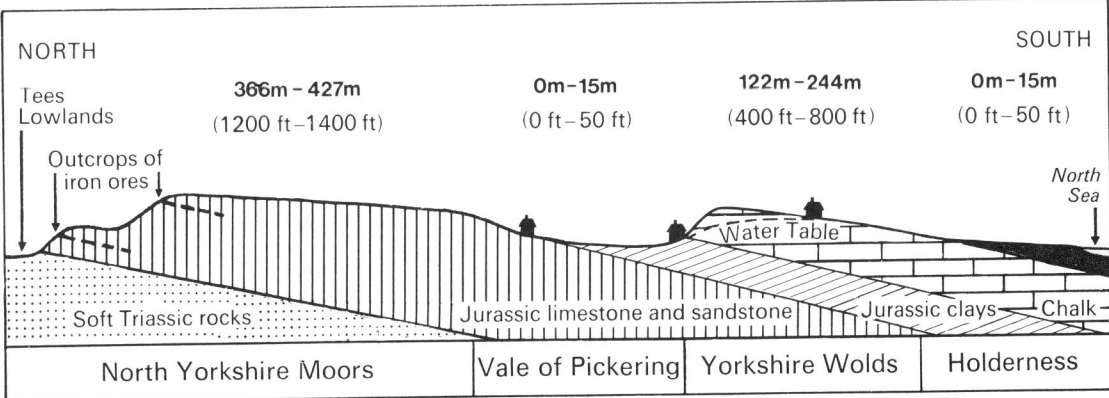

Work to do

1. Study the first map on page 28 (Map B (a)) and suggest reasons for the following names: Springfield House (956765); Westfield House (946766); White Gate (954756); Cow Pasture Gate (957776); Cut Bridge (956784); Ings Farm (947792).
2. Sketch a relief profile from north to south across the first map on page 28 (Map B (a)) through Westfield House. On the section add the names: flat floor of the Vale of Pickering; steep scarp slope of Yorkshire Wolds. Mark and name: the River Derwent; old course of the river; the railway; the A64; Westfield House; the spring at 946761; the dry valley which leaves the edge of the map at 953740.
3. Compare the areas north and south of the A64 road on Map B(a) and show how they differ. Use the headings: geology; relief; drainage; land use.
4. Make a table to show the work at Westfield Farm month by month throughout the year. Compare it with the one for Lowlands Farm (Chapter 1) and with one for a farm in your home area.
5. Make a pie graph to show the crops grown at Westfield Farm. (Note: a pie graph is shown in Chapter 5).
6. Fig 46 shows the stages in the making of steel at B.S.C.'s works in Scunthorpe. Notice how there are various inputs into the works (e.g., iron ore) and outputs at the end of the process (finished steel). The output from one stage in the process becomes the input for the next. The workings of a farm can be represented in a similar way. Make such a diagram for Westfield Farm. You can begin by making a list of all the inputs (e.g. fertilisers and seed) and the outputs (e.g. bacon pigs and cereals). Then put them into an annotated diagram to show how the farming system at Westfield Farm works.
7. Make a similar diagram for Lowlands Farm and compare the two.
8. Make a sketch or tracing of Fig 27. On it mark and name: the flat top of the plateau; the steep valley sides; the flat valley floor; the bare outcrops of rock; the railway. Add the title 'A glacial channel in the North York Moors'.
9. Make a copy of the section across East Yorkshire (Fig 28). Underneath make a table of notes for each area under the headings: geology; relief; drainage; land use.
10. The decision to allow drilling for oil and natural gas on the North York Moors and the opening of the potash mine at Boulby aroused opposition from people who wished to conserve the natural beauty of the National Park. Decisions such as these often follow a public enquiry in which all the interested parties are allowed to present their case. Conduct a mock public enquiry on this or a similar controversial planning problem with different groups of pupils preparing and presenting the evidence of the various interested parties.

4 | THE YORKSHIRE COAST

29 *Coastal erosion at Skipsea*

The Scenery of the Yorkshire Coast

One of the thrills of visiting the seaside is the sight of waves breaking on the shore, especially when the sea is rough. But stormy seas can have given no pleasure to the owners of holiday bungalows overhanging the edge of the low cliff in the photograph (Fig 29). For many years along this stretch of coastline people have been striving to save their houses and holiday bungalows by building sea walls but these are continually swept away by the waves. Each year more houses topple into the sea.

This is not a new problem along the Holderness coast of Yorkshire where erosion has been going on for centuries. Since Roman times a strip of land three to five kilometres (two to three miles) wide has been swept away by the sea and whole villages have been lost (Fig 30). This is because the coast south of Bridlington is made of soft boulder-clay which is so easily worn away by the waves that the coast is moving inland at

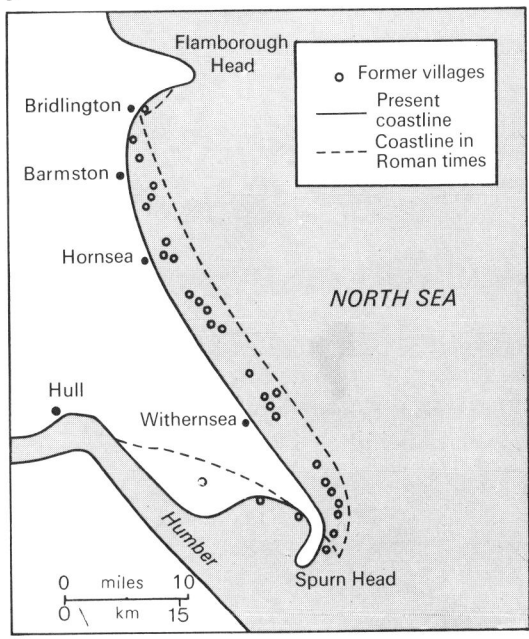

30 *Coastal erosion in Holderness*

33

the rate of about two metres (six to seven feet) a year. The effect of the severe summer drought of 1976, followed by a winter of heavy rain and frost, is reported to have increased the rate of erosion even more.

The sea is constantly moving the sand and pebbles it has washed out of the cliffs. As a wave breaks an uprush of water carries material up the beach and the backwash moves some of it down again. The diagram (Fig 31) shows what happens when the waves approach the coast at an angle. Notice how the pebble follows a zig-zag path along the beach. Such a movement of material is known as longshore drifting. On the Yorkshire coast, where waves frequently come from the north-east driven by easterly winds, longshore drifting is from north to south. A small amount of the beach material transported in this way is deposited at the mouth of the Humber to form the sand spit at Spurn Head. This is a long, narrow, curving strip of land which widens at its southern end. A lighthouse warns ships sailing up the Humber of the exact position of this dangerous headland.

Further north the coast juts out into the North Sea at Flamborough Head. The white rock seen at the bottom of the cliffs in the photograph (Fig 32) is chalk. Three hundred kilometres (two hundred miles) away on the south coast similar rocks form the famous white cliffs of Dover. Chalk is more resistant to the waves than the softer clays to the north and south which have been cut into by the sea to form bays. Many of the bays and headlands at the coast result from the arrangement of harder and softer rocks.

Even the chalk does not escape completely from the attack of the sea. Waves find their way into cracks and joints and carve gulleys out of the cliffs. These are widened to form caves and in time part of a small headland may be cut through to form an arch. Eventually the top of the arch may collapse leaving pinnacles of rock called stacks which in time are also destroyed by the waves. Thus the whole cliff is moving slowly inland and one day the lighthouse may be in a similar position to the bungalows in Fig 29. Rocks which are partly covered by the sea can be seen in the picture at the bottom of the cliffs and along the edge of the beach at the head of the small bay. These are the remains of cliffs which at one time stood further out into the sea.

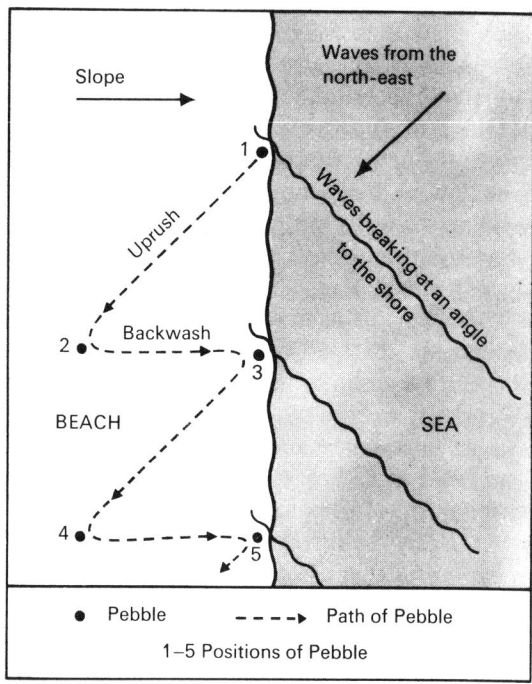

31 *Longshore drifting*

High rocky cliffs like those at Flamborough are found further north along the Yorkshire coast where the hard rocks of the North York Moors reach the sea. These form one of the longest stretches of cliff coast in Britain. They are broken in a few places such as Robin Hood's Bay where softer rocks have been worn away by the waves. Low cliffs like those of Holderness are found around Filey Bay and along the north coast between Saltburn and the Tees.

Whitby, a holiday resort in North Yorkshire

Marked on the street plan of Whitby (Fig 33) is a small fish and chip restaurant. Notice how it is situated close to the harbour in the busy centre of the town. In winter the customers are mainly local people and business is quiet enough for the owners to shut the cafe by mid-afternoon and stay closed at weekends. This gives them a chance to prepare for the summer when the town is so crowded with visitors that they are busy seven days a week cooking and serving meals until late in the evenings. At this time of the year there are usually a number of paying guests staying with them in their house above the cafe because the owners are also boarding house keepers.

The town's holiday guide advertises about thirty other boarding houses as well as hotels, guest houses, holiday flats, caravan sites and camping grounds. Catering for visitors has become the main occupation of the people who live in Whitby and the other holiday resorts on the Yorkshire coast.

The photograph (Fig 34) shows how Whitby looks from the air. Notice the piers at the entrance to the harbour, the steep cliffs and the sands. See also how the town lies in a sheltered position at the mouth of a valley carved out of the plateau by the River Esk. These features of the town, together with others shown on the street plan, help to explain why there are over a quarter of a million visitors to Whitby each summer. Most of them come from the industrial towns of the West Riding and Teesside either for their holidays or for a day at the seaside.

Whitby has not always been a holiday resort. Before the opening of the railway from Pickering across the North York Moors in 1837, people found it difficult even to reach the town. How different from today when motor cars, coaches and trains enable people to travel long distances to spend just a day by the sea. For many centuries Whitby was a great seaport. The monuments to Captain Cook marked on the street plan remind visitors of this. It was from Whitby that he set off on his voyages of discovery round the world in the eighteenth century. In the town is an arch of whale jaw bones, big enough to walk through, which is a relic of the times when wooden boats sailed from Whitby to the waters off Greenland to catch whales. A hundred and thirty sailing ships were built in the town in 1706 when Whitby was the biggest port

32 *The cliffs at Flamborough Head*

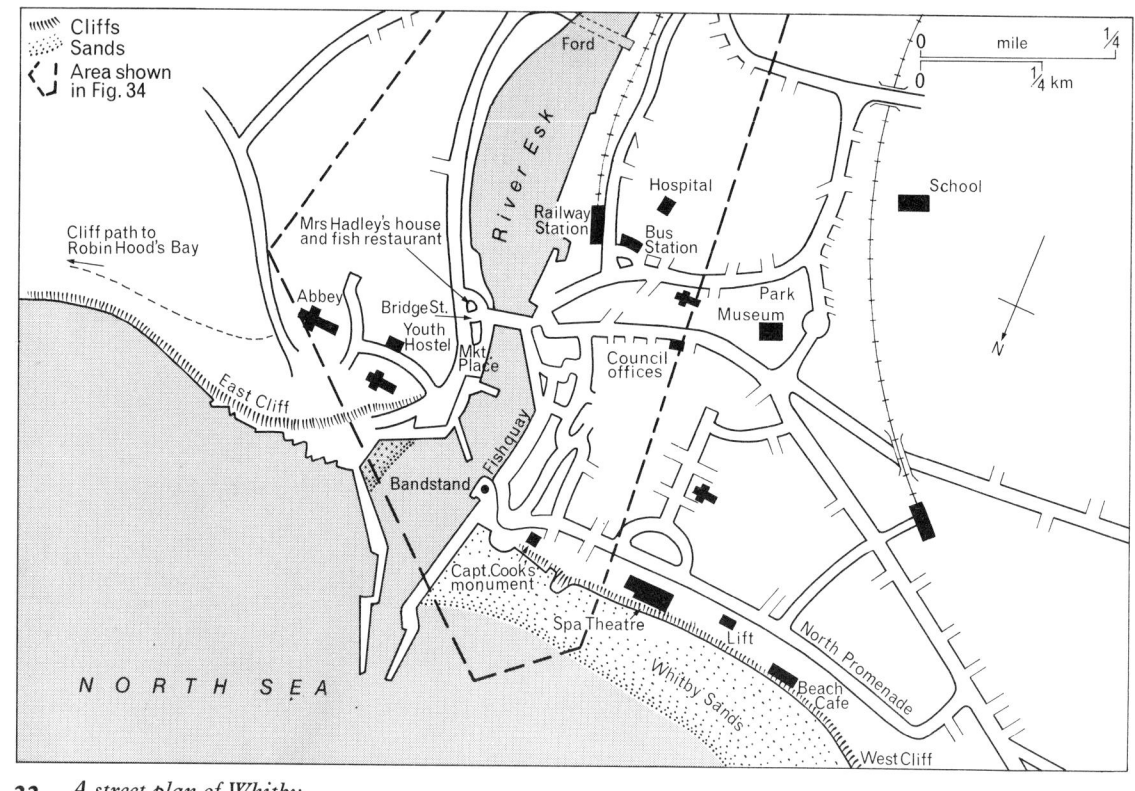

33 *A street plan of Whitby*

34 *Whitby from the air*

on the Yorkshire coast and the sixth in the whole of Britain.

Whitby harbour is still busy, though today it is small compared with Hull and other large ports. Notice on the map (Fig 35) how it is divided into the Upper and Lower Harbours at the Swing Bridge. Usually the fishing boats land about £700,000 worth of fish a year in the Lower Harbour where the Fish Quay, Market and Pier are found together with the Lifeboat Station and the office of the Harbour Master. In the Upper Harbour is Endeavour Wharf where boats of up to 2,000 tonnes can load and unload their cargoes. Note that it is situated next to the railway sidings, and that storage yards and sheds have been built alongside for timber. Steel (to Belgium), general cargo (to the Black Sea) and insulating paper (to Russia) are the chief exports which amounted to 19,000 tonnes in 1976. Steel (from Holland), rice pellets and grain (also from Holland) and timber (from Norway) are the main imports, which totalled 136,000 tonnes in 1976.

On the eastern side of the Upper Harbour is the boat yard of Whitby Ship-building Company. The slipway, built in 1963, is used for launching ships of up to 810 tonnes (800 tons). A small industrial estate has recently been developed alongside the Whitby/Scarborough road. Unlike the tourist industry, this provides work throughout the year for local people.

Scarborough Harbour
Further south on the Yorkshire coast at Scarborough is a much larger resort and fishing port than Whitby. It claims to have over a million visitors a year. The town has many attractions including its busy harbour.

Small open fishing boats known as cobbles are frequently used in the summer for taking visitors on a trip round the bay. They are also used for inshore fishing especially in summer for lobsters and crabs which are caught in 'pots'. These are small traps which are baited with pieces of fish and lowered to the seabed at points along the coast. They are pulled back to the surface by lines tied to marker buoys. The fishermen also catch cod, haddock, skate and ling from the cobbles using long lines with baited hooks.

Scarborough harbour also has a fleet of about thirty keelboats which are used for fishing in the

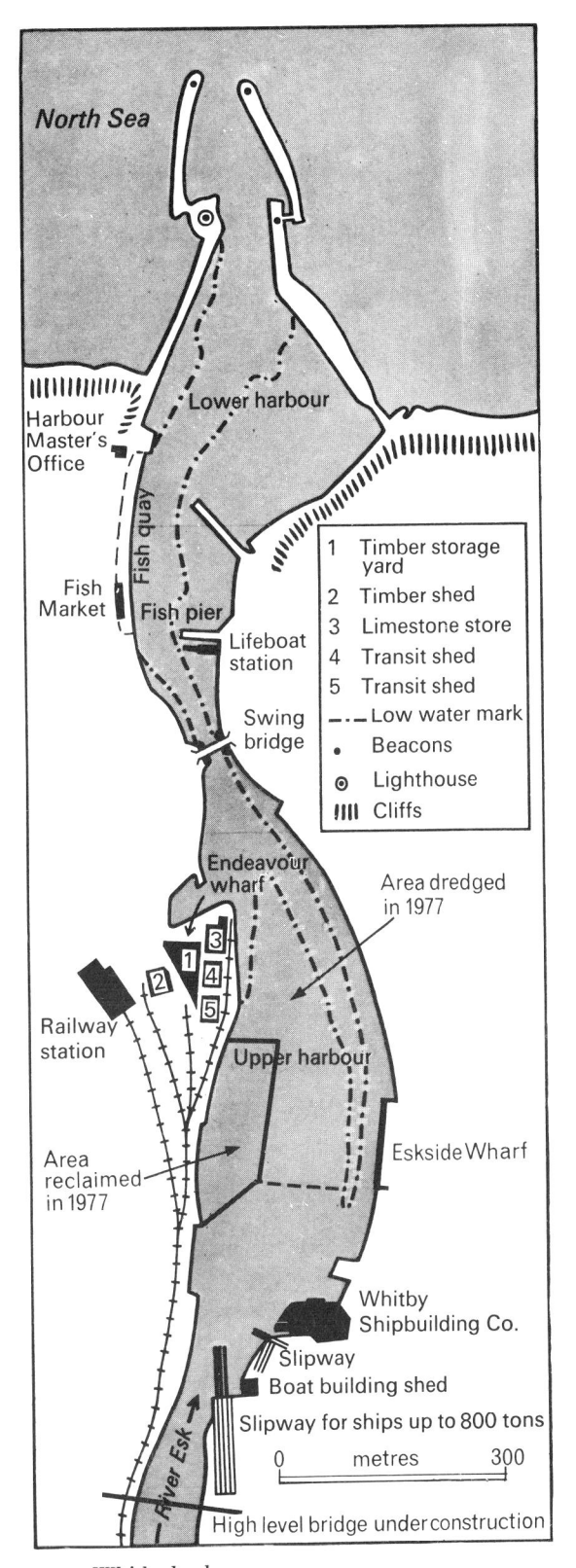

35 *Whitby harbour*

36 *Whitby harbour*

North Sea. The keelboats fish with a trawl net which is pulled along the seabed by the boat and is kept open by the otter boards. By this means, the catch includes fish like plaice, sole, cod and haddock which swim near the bottom of the sea.

Scarborough was once a famous herring fishing port and was visited annually by a fleet of over one hundred 'drifters' which moved southwards from Scotland to East Anglia following the huge shoals of fish. As a result of over-fishing, the herring has almost disappeared from the North Sea and few, if any, Scottish boats come south today. The shortage has become so acute that in 1977 the British government imposed a ban on herring fishing within 200 miles of the coast.

At Scarborough the fishing boats land about £1,500,000 worth of fish a year at the Fish Market Pier. There it is auctioned to buyers who send it by refrigerated road transport to West Yorkshire, Lancashire, the Midlands and London.

Above the seafront is Scarborough Castle on a high headland which protects the harbour from north easterly gales. Close to the harbour are the houses and cottages of the old fishing port. Many are now holiday houses while the buildings along the sea front have been converted into shops, cafes and amusement arcades. The town has grown inland and along the coast to become Yorkshire's largest holiday resort.

Work to do

1. Study Fig 32 and suggest reasons why people visit Flamborough Head. Include in your answer both natural and man-made features.
2. Read pages 33 and 34 and then draw an input–output diagram to represent the effects of the sea on the Holderness Coast.
3. Read page 34 and then draw a diagram to show the development of caves, arches and stacks.

4. Explain why the severe drought in the summer of 1976 followed by a winter of heavy rain and frost increased the rate of erosion of the Holderness coast.
5. Design a holiday poster or brochure of the Yorkshire coast, illustrating its attractions including those of the main resorts.
6. In recent years catches of fish off the Yorkshire coast, particularly herring, have declined because of overfishing. Make lists of (a) the possible reasons for overfishing and (b) possible solutions to the problem.
7. Write a paragraph on the changes of scenery you would see on a journey along the coast of Yorkshire from the mouth of the Tees to Spurn Head.
8. Make a map of the coastline of Yorkshire. On it mark and name: (a) the holiday resorts of Redcar, Whitby, Robin Hood's Bay, Scarborough, Filey and Bridlington; (b) the direction of longshore drifting; (c) the main bays and headlands; (d) the Tees and Humber. Add a suitable title.
9. From other sources of information, such as holiday brochures, make a table of the facilities and attractions offered by the coastal holiday resorts of Yorkshire. Hold a discussion or organise a questionaire to discover which resort people would most like to visit.
10. Study the diagram below and then write a comparison of the drifting and trawling methods of fishing.

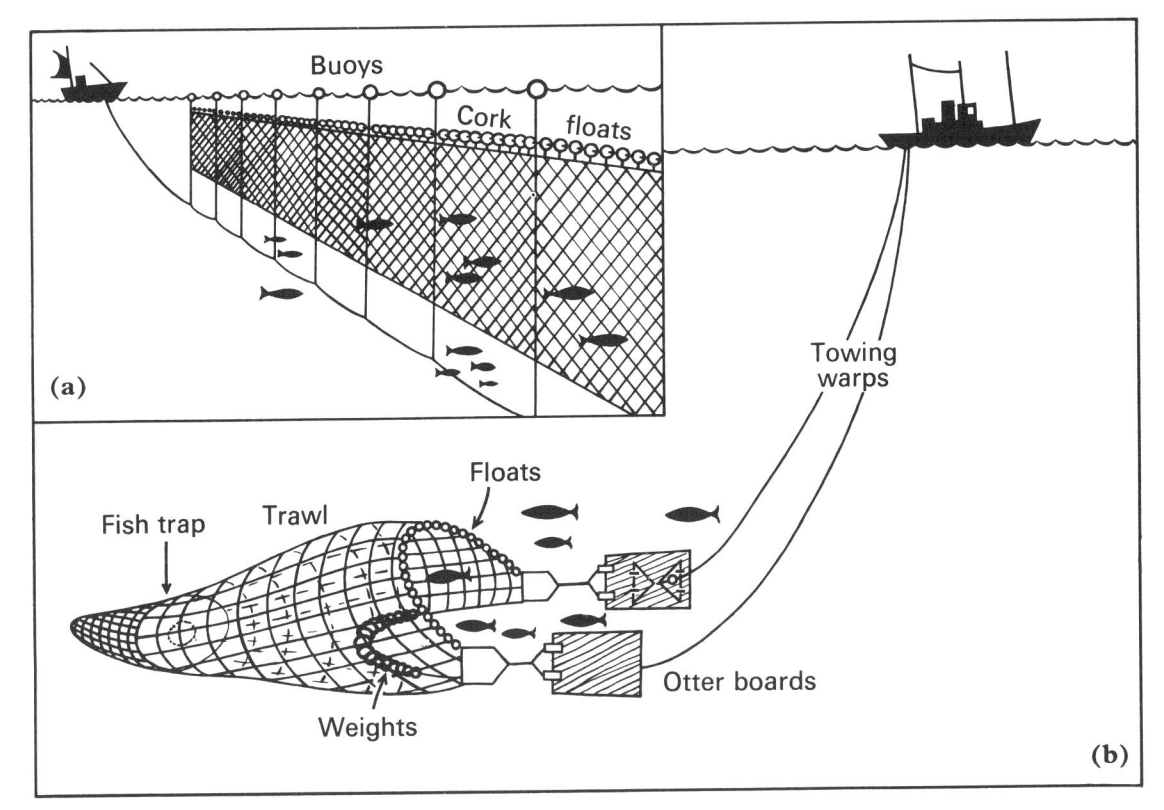

(a) Drifting, once used for catching herring
(b) Trawling, used for catching fish which swim near the sea bed

5 | HUMBERSIDE

Charting the Humber Channel

Each day the small motor boat 'Conservancy' sets out from Brough on the River Humber, 55 km (35 miles) from its mouth on the North Sea. For about four hours the crew of five men work their way from side to side across the river measuring and recording the depth of the bed along survey lines spaced 90 metres (300 feet) apart. When they have completed their survey the information is plotted onto a chart; if any changes have occurred, ships are warned immediately and buoys and lights are moved to mark the new position of the deep channel.

Daily surveys like those carried out from Brough cover the whole of the Humber estuary and its approaches. They are important because the navigable channel of the river is constantly changing its course; it has been known to shift 150 metres (500 feet) in two weeks. These changes in the river-bed are caused by the deposition of vast amounts of mud. Some people think that these have been washed up the estuary by tides from Holderness. Others argue that the mud has been brought down from the Pennines and North York Moors by the tributaries of the Humber.

Despite the careful watch which is kept on the channel, large ships would not be able to navigate the upper reaches of the Humber but for the high tides which twice a day deepen the water in the river. For a period of about three hours before and up to high water ships as large as 3,000 tonnes can navigate the river between Goole and the North Sea. Although a jetty is provided at Blacktoft for moorings, modern ships are generally fast enough to make the passage in the time available.

The Inland Port of Goole

Goole is the most inland port on the east coast of Britain; to reach it, ships sail eighty kilometres (fifty miles) along the Humber and the Yorkshire Ouse from the North Sea.

The docks were first opened in 1826 by the Aire and Calder Navigation Company as the terminus for a canal system which linked industrial towns of West Yorkshire and a large area of the Yorkshire coalfield with the North Sea via the Humber estuary. Today the waterways serving Goole and the ports on the Humber estuary are the most important in Britain after the Manchester Ship Canal. The map (Fig 37) shows that Goole is situated where the River Don meets the Yorkshire Ouse, about thirteen kilometres (eight miles) east of where the New Junction Canal meets the Aire and Calder Navigation. The canal and waterway system, which is owned by the British Waterways Board, carries about 3 million tonnes of cargo a year, much of it coal and coal

37 *The inland waterways serving the Humber Ports*

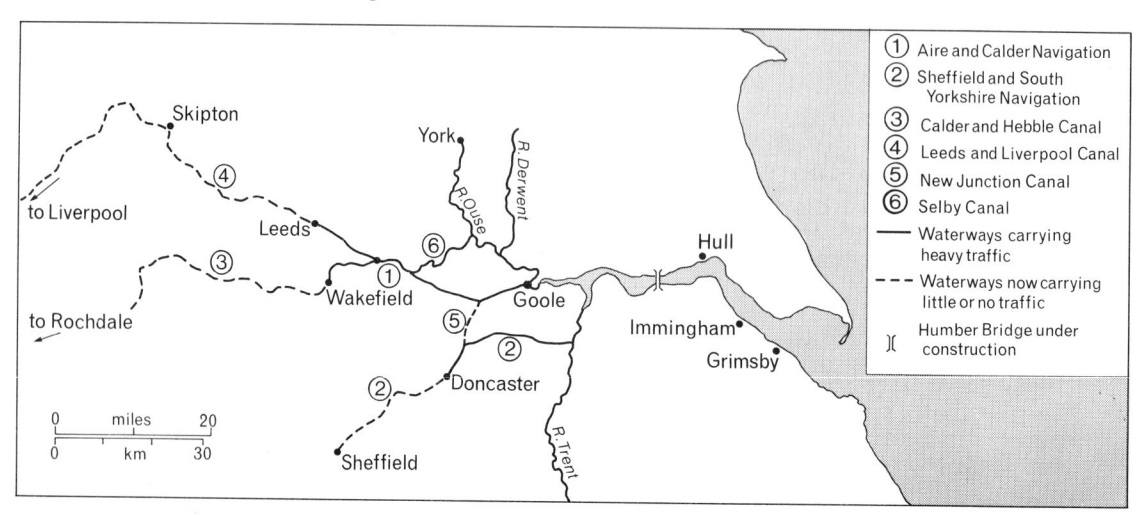

38 *A push–tow composite craft on the Aire–Calder Navigation near Castleford*

products going to power stations or to Goole for export.

The strange boat shown in Fig 38 is a push–tow craft. The three 'sections' full of coal can be pushed or pulled by the small but powerful tug. These manoeuvrable craft can carry 700 tonnes of coal. They work between the collieries near Castleford and the Knottingley power stations. Notice the width of the navigation, the stonework protecting the banks and the Permian Limestone scarp in the distance. Today, about 40 per cent of the coal exported from Goole goes there by water. It is carried there in special compartment boats called 'Tom Puddings' each of which carry about 40 tonnes of coal. The rest is transported by rail.

The plan of Goole docks (Fig 39) shows the position of the tipping hoists which are used to tip the coal direct from the compartment boats and railway wagons into waiting colliers. Notice also the three locks which keep the water in the fifteen hectares (thirty-seven acres) of docks at a constant depth of six metres (twenty feet) by preventing the level from rising and falling with the tides in the River Ouse. Ships and barges entering the port must first pass through the locks. Once inside there are eight docks with a total of five kilometres (three miles) of quayside at which they can berth. Beside the docks are transit sheds where cargo is stored, many of which are equipped with overhead cranes. Ship repairing is carried out in Goole's dry docks.

Notice in Table 1 that the exports of coal

Table 1.   *The Trade of Goole 1976*

Imports	
Commodity	*Tonnes*
Cereals and grain	122,158
Dairy products and other foodstuffs	26,185
Timber, wood and paper manufactures	155,248
Wool textiles and fibres	9,967
Metal ores	18,122
Building materials	9,433
Petroleum and products	2,842
Chemicals and chemical fertilisers	71,221
Iron and steel goods (including scrap)	435,578
Machinery and vehicles	28,943
Other commodities	31,385
Total imports	911,082

Exports	
Commodity	*Tonnes*
Foostuffs	15,982
Building materials (including pitch)	23,990
Chemicals and chemical fertilisers	31,300
Textiles and fabrics	16,726
Iron and steel goods (including scrap)	64,658
Machinery, vehicles and spare parts	48,639
Coal, coke and patent fuel	590,509
Other commodities	192,543
Total exports	984,257

and coal products amount to just under one third of the total trade of the port. For many

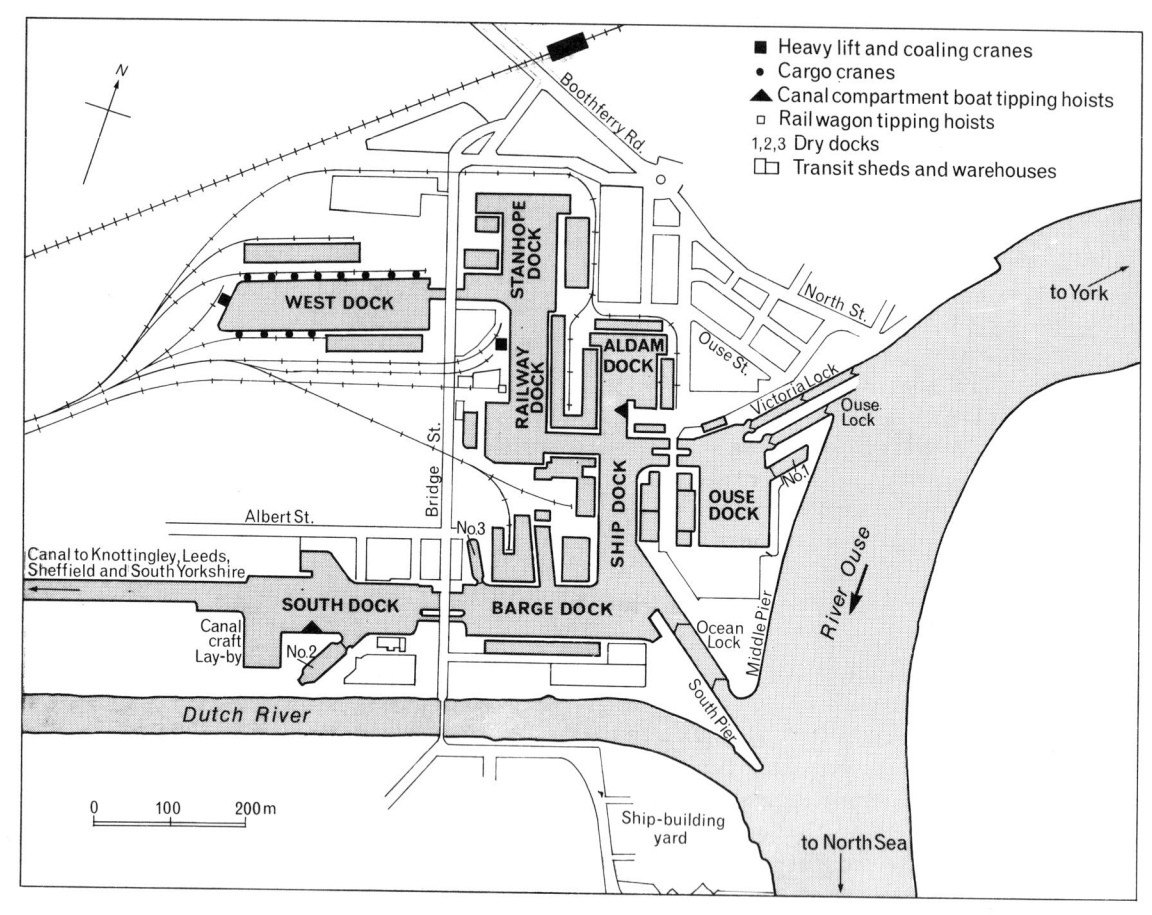

39 *A plan of Goole docks*

years coal and coke accounted for sixty to eighty per cent of the total trade but the increase in the use of oil and North Sea gas has dramatically reduced this proportion while trade in general cargo has substantially increased. Today the tonnage of general cargo now handled at Goole is the highest in the port's history.

Most of the coal and coke is exported to Europe, Scandinavia being the main customer, and about twenty per cent of the coal exported is house coal which goes to British ports.

Goole has regular cargo liner services to Norway, Sweden, Finland, Germany, Holland, Belgium, France, Spain, Morocco and South Africa. There is also trade by charter vessel to and from many other countries, including Russia, Denmark, Italy and the Mediterranean. Cargo from other parts of the world, such as the U.S.A., China and Australia reaches Goole by transhipment services from Rotterdam.

The main imports are grain, timber, fertilisers and iron and steel goods. Exports apart from coal and coke include whisky, pitch, chemicals, textiles, iron and steel goods, caravans, tractors, agricultural machinery and spare parts.

When Goole first opened as a port it was a small new village of 450 people. Now it is a small town with about 18,000 inhabitants.

The International Seaport of Hull

Forty kilometres (twenty-five miles) downstream from Goole, where the River Hull flows into the wide estuary of the Humber, is the great seaport of Hull. The city's full name is Kingston-upon-

Hull meaning 'the King's town' because in 1293 it was a new town built as a port by Edward I. Now about five million tonnes of cargo pass through its docks each year making it one of the largest seaports in Britain.

The map (Fig 40) shows Hull in 1640. Notice the small size of the town and how it was surrounded by walls and moats. These enabled Hull to withstand two sieges by Royalists during the Civil War; they also protected it from flooding by the high tides of the Humber. The larger ships were anchored in the sheltered inlet formed by the River Hull and the Humber was used only by smaller ships. The plan of the port as it is today (Fig 41) shows that the old harbour at the mouth of the River Hull is no longer important and that the docks stretch for eleven kilometres (seven miles) along the north bank of the Humber.

King George Dock with an area of twenty-five hectares (sixty-two acres) and over three kilometres (two miles) of quayside, is the largest of the six docks. A huge silo capable of holding 60,000 tonnes of grain stands at its western end. Alongside its quays are vast transit sheds where cargo from all parts of the world is stored. In one of them bales of wool from New Zealand wait to be delivered to woollen mills in the West Riding. One third of all the wool imported into Britain arrives at Hull, most of it at King George Dock. Two of the quays are equipped to handle timber, ores and iron and steel goods which do not need to be stored inside transit sheds. It is not unusual to see British motor cars, lorries, buses and tractors parked in the open at the dockside waiting to be shipped overseas. In recent years the dock has been improved by the building of roll-on/roll-off terminals where cars and lorries can be driven on and off the boats without using cranes.

Close to the mouth of the River Hull were the Victoria, Princess, Railway, and Humber Docks which have now been closed. Alexandra Dock has been extensively modernised to include the provision of new berths, cranes, sheds, storage facilities and parking areas. This dock caters for ocean going vessels and short sea trades. At the modern Riverside Quay, passengers depart for ports on the North Sea.

At the eastern end of the port, at Saltend, three jetties reach 490 metres (1,600 feet) into the

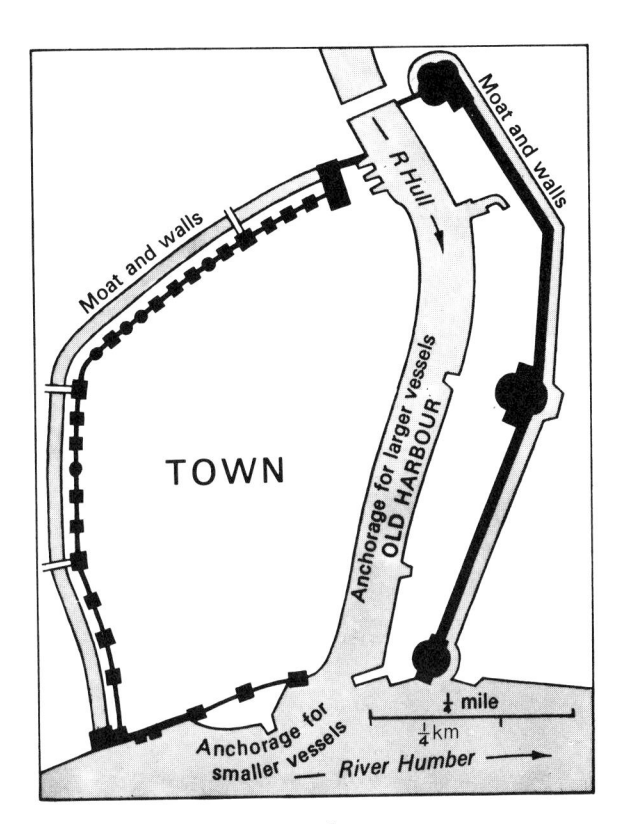

40 *Kingston-upon-Hull 1640*

River Humber. Here ocean-going tankers of 35,000 tonnes pipe ashore cargoes of oil, alcohol, molasses and chemicals. Hull's imports of oil amount to over 750,000 tonnes a year. St Andrew's Dock, occupied by the fishing industry since 1883, has now been closed and modern facilities have been provided in the Albert and William Wright Docks. Hull first became important for fishing in the nineteenth century when the Dogger Banks were discovered. However, there are now only 35 fishing vessels registered at Hull the majority of which freeze their catch at sea. Since they have been banned from their traditional fishing grounds in the North Atlantic Hull's fishermen have turned to catching mackerel off the coast of Cornwall. However, very little 'wet' (as opposed as 'frozen') fish is now landed at Hull. In 1979 only 147 vessels landed unfrozen fish at the port and of these only 12 were registered at Hull, the rest being mainly Icelandic. As a result the quayside auctions of fish are smaller in scale and less frequent than they used to be. The reduced size of Hull's fishing fleet and smaller fish landings have led to a fall in the number of people employed in the fishing industry and hence to a rise in unemployment.

How different this is from the Middle Ages when Hull's trade was mainly the export of corn and wool from the farmlands of the East Riding! The big changes occurred in the eighteenth and nineteenth centuries when new towns and industries began to develop. The Midlands and the North needed a port through which they could export their products and import food and raw materials in return. Communications to Hull were improved, first by the cutting of canals, and later by the building of railways and the improvement of roads. Large new docks had to be built along the Humber for the big steamers which replaced the small wooden sailing ships. Hull extended its hinterland to include West and South Yorkshire, Lancashire, 'the Potteries', 'the Black Country' and the North Midlands.

The circular diagrams (Fig 42) are called pie graphs because they are divided into segments like a pie. They show that although ships from all parts of the world dock at Hull, much of its trade is with the countries of Europe especially those bordering the North Sea. These countries are the destination of over three quarters of Hull's exports and the origin of about a half of its imports. The graphs also show that the imported

Table 2. *The Trade of Hull 1976*

Imports

Commodity	Tonnes
Cereals	135,137
Foodstuffs	541,278
Timber	237,490
Ores	79,774
Wool and textile fibres	41,933
Oilseed and nuts	127,264
Petroleum	570,830
Other commodities	1,551,413
Fish landings	93,213
Total imports (including coastwise)	3,378,342

Exports

Commodity	Tonnes
Foodstuffs	118,189
Chemicals and fertilisers	412,051
Iron and steel goods	173,945
Machinery and vehicles	196,215
Textiles	72,983
Coal and coke	1,215
Petroleum	83,286
Bunker fuel (petroleum)	93,399
Other commodities	829,575
Total exports (including coastwise)	1,980,858

41 *A plan of Hull Docks*

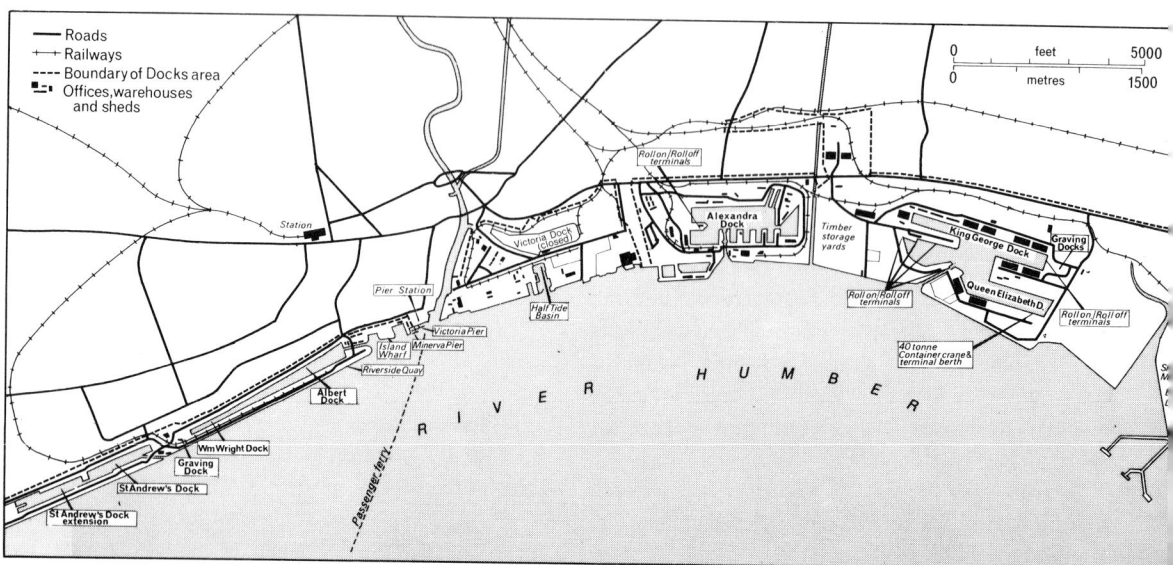

IMPORTS INTO HULL (1976)

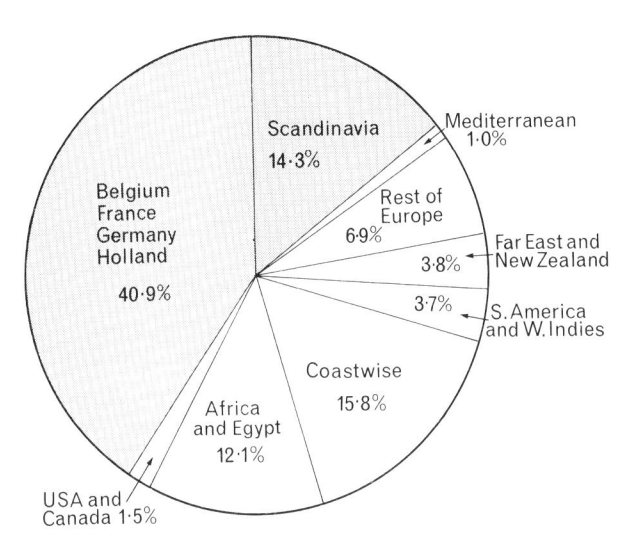

Belgium France Germany Holland 40.9%
Scandinavia 14.3%
Mediterranean 1.0%
Rest of Europe 6.9%
Far East and New Zealand 3.8%
S. America and W. Indies 3.7%
Coastwise 15.8%
Africa and Egypt 12.1%
USA and Canada 1.5%

Total 3.3 million tonnes

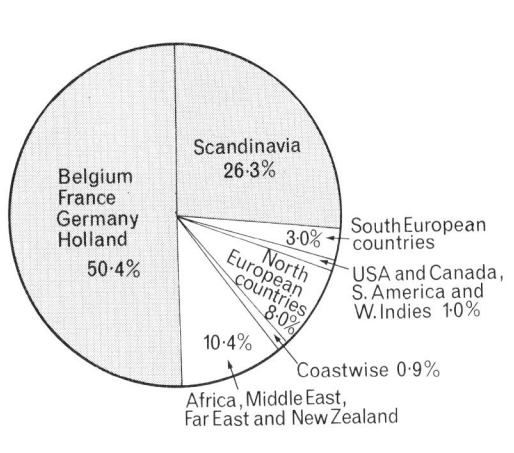

EXPORTS FROM HULL (1976)

Belgium France Germany Holland 50.4%
Scandinavia 26.3%
South European countries 3.0%
USA and Canada, S. America and W. Indies 1.0%
North European countries 8.0%
Coastwise 0.9%
Africa, Middle East, Far East and New Zealand 10.4%

Total 1.8 million tonnes

42 *The direction of Hull's trade*

cargoes by weight are nearly twice those which are exported. As Table 2 shows, this is because Hull imports large amounts of food and industrial raw materials whereas most of its exports are manufactured goods.

As well as being a great port, Hull is a busy industrial city with a population of about 277,000. Most of its factories are found by the docks along the Hull and Humber rivers. Many of them have their own wharves where 'lighters' or small river boats can unload cargoes of raw materials brought from ships berthed in the main docks. Huge grain mills where the heart of the wheat is separated from the husk are typical of the factories which stand on the banks of the River Hull. Some of the grain used is British, but most of it comes from Australia, Canada, U.S.A. and Argentina. Oilseed and rice milling, paint and cement making, shipbuilding and repairing, tar distilling, tanning and chemicals are other industries found alongside the River Hull near the old part of the town. By the River Humber at Saltend on the outskirts of Hull is a new industrial estate where oil is used for making paints, plastics and textile fibres.

The Bulk Cargo Port of Immingham

Sixteen kilometres (ten miles) downstream from Hull on the south side of the Humber is the Lincolnshire port of Immingham. Table 3 shows that bulky cargoes of metal ores, chemicals

Table 3. *The Trade of Immingham 1976*

Imports	
Commodity	*Tonnes*
Foodstuffs	102,693
Timber	45,024
Iron ore and roasted pyrites	4,920,850
Non-ferrous ores	332,402
Chemicals and fertilisers	1,464,568
Building materials and crude minerals	45,975
Iron and steel	541,505
Petroleum	8,586,207
Other commodities	418,385
Total imports	16,457,609

Exports	
Commodity	*Tonnes*
Foodstuffs	26,503
Basic materials	42,118
Chemicals and fertilisers	509,891
Iron and steel goods	618,433
Machinery and vehicles	152,952
Coal	436,217
Petroleum	4,681,061
Other commodities	259,772
Total exports	6,726,947

and petroleum are the chief commodities which pass through the port.

The docks, which are shown in the plan (Fig 43), cover twenty hectares (fifty acres) and have about 2,100 metres (7,000 feet) of quayside. Ships enter the port from the Humber through a lock which is 256 metres (840 feet) long and 27 metres (90 feet) wide. Four jetties reach out into the deep channel of the Humber which swings close to the south side of the estuary at this point. The largest tankers to navigate the Humber discharge their cargoes of oil from Venezuela and the Middle East and chemicals from North Africa, U.S.A. and Germany at the Immingham oil terminal.

Close by along the banks of the river are large areas of storage tanks belonging to well-known petrol companies. Imported chemicals such as sulphur and phosphates are made into fertilisers by Fisons at their factory alongside the docks. Other chemical works on Humberside between Immingham and Grimsby are supplied with raw materials from the port.

One of the most remarkable features of the port is the facilities at the National Coal Board and British Steel Corporation jetty for the export of coal and the import of iron ore. Here a coal vessel can be loaded simultaneously with the unloading of a 100,000 tonne ore carrier. Trains carrying 1,600 tonnes transport the Brazilian and Swedish iron ore to the steel works at Scunthorpe thirty kilometres (nineteen miles) away. The coal is brought by rail from Nottinghamshire and South Yorkshire for export. Table 3 shows that petroleum, finished iron and steel goods and chemicals and fertilisers are important in Immingham's export trade.

The position of Immingham on the south side of the Humber gives it an advantage over Hull for serving the collieries and industrial towns of the Midlands.

The Fishing Port of Grimsby

Grimsby is one of the world's greatest fishing ports. In 1976 nearly 3,000 men were working from the Grimsby fish docks but the industry is now in decline as a result of the fall in stocks of fish in the North Sea and the 200 mile fishing limit imposed around the coast of Iceland. Grimsby fishermen used to sail to the North Atlantic and Arctic Oceans, voyages of forty days not being uncommon with the catches being frozen at sea.

Large cold stores and processing factories have been built in Grimsby like the one shown in the photograph (Fig 44). Here fish is being filleted and weighed before being put into packets and frozen ready for distribution to the shops in refrigerated lorries. Grimsby is now the centre of Britain's frozen foods industry. Vegetables, fruit and other foodstuffs in addition to fish are frozen in factories belonging to 'Bird's Eye', 'Ross' and other well-known companies. Many of the vegetables such as peas and beans are grown by Lincolnshire farmers under contract to these companies.

Table 4 shows that Grimsby, unlike Hull and Immingham, handles mainly general cargo. This is because the approach waters to the port are too shallow for the bulk cargo ships which dock at Hull and Immingham.

Table 4.   *The Trade of Grimsby 1976*

Imports	
Commercial docks	
Commodity	*Tonnes*
Dairy produce	58,318
Other foodstuffs	273,490
Timber	97,335
Iron and steel	139,013
Machinery and vehicles	24,890
Other manufactured goods	91,944
Fish landings	107,675
Petroleum	32,500
Other commodities	152,880
Total imports	978,045

Exports	
Commodity	*Tonnes*
Foodstuffs	14,724
Basic materials	25,094
Chemicals	34,603
Iron and steel goods	63,370
Machinery and vehicles	31,278
Other manufactured goods	61,486
Other commodities	247,196
Total exports	477,751

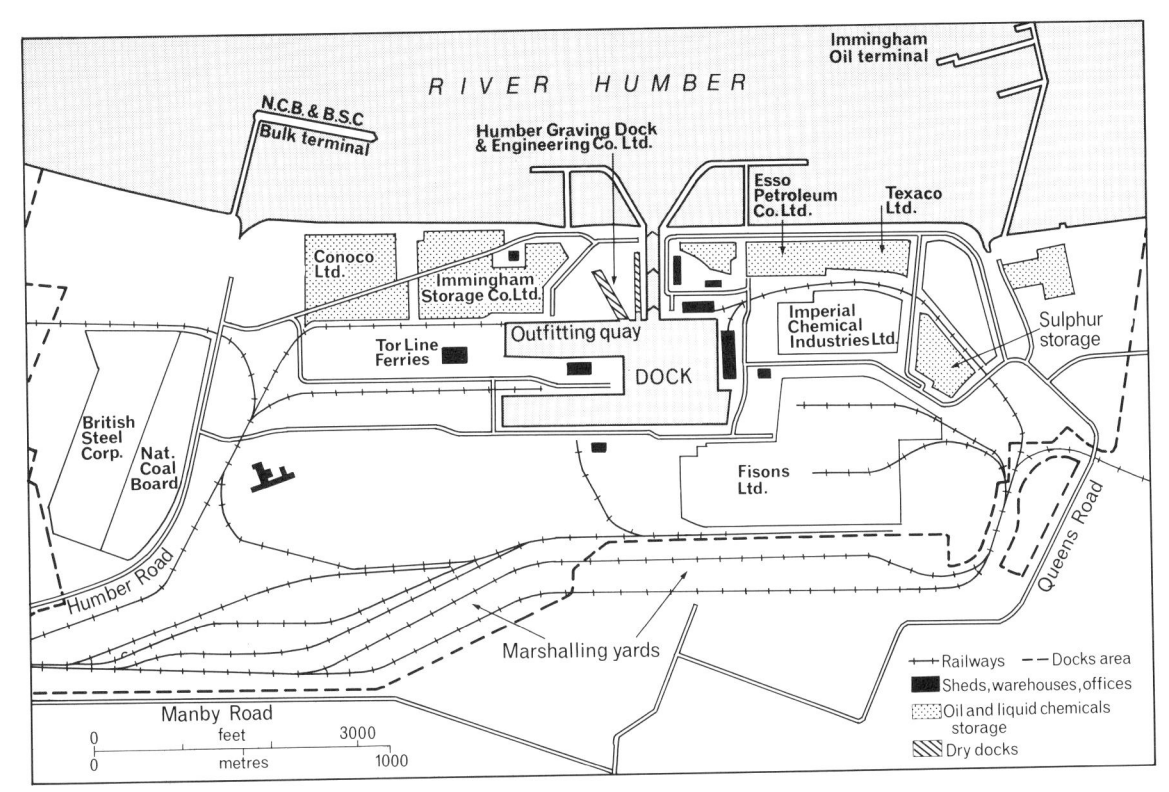

43 *A plan of Immingham Docks*

Development on Humberside

While in the early 1970s newspaper headlines quite frequently announced proposals for development schemes on either side of the Humber to encourage new industries in the area, progress over the last few years has slowed down.

However some of the developments which have already taken place are those to the south of the river at Immingham where the biggest fertiliser plant in Europe and the Lindsey oil refinery belonging to the 'Continental Oil Company' have been built. Nearby at Killingholme 'Total-Petrofina' have built another and tankers with capacities of up to 260,000 tonnes often discharge cargoes of 120,000 tonnes of crude oil alongside the jetties at Immingham. North of the Humber in Yorkshire millions of pounds have been spent on modernising the port of Hull, while at Easington on Spurn Head a terminal has been built where the first supplies of natural gas from the North Sea were brought ashore by underwater pipeline.

The residents of Humberside who now cross the river by a ferryboat between Hull and New Holland will soon be able to do so by the new Humber Bridge which has been talked about for over a hundred years and which it is estimated will be completed by the end of 1980. Planners claim that when the bridge is finished workers from Hull will be able to reach the industries on the south side in about half an hour. At present many people who wish to cross the river do so by travelling many kilometres inland to Boothferry Bridge near Goole. On the south side of the Humber, the linkroads between Immingham and Grimsby and the present end of the M18, west of the River Trent, are narrow and congested. However, Hull is linked by a dual carriage-way to the M62 which now extends east of the River Ouse since the completion of a new bridge just north of Goole.

Despite the disadvantages of its communication links with its hinterland which are now being overcome, Humberside offers many opportunities to new industries. It is particularly favourable to those which import large quantities of raw materials and which trade with Europe. Bulk cargoes of oil and chemicals can be imported up the deep channel of the Humber and the low flat land beside the estuary gives ideal sites for large factories. Labour is also available, especially since the trawlers lost their right to fish in many waters around Iceland leading to a general decline in the fishing industry and a rise in unemployment. Supplies of water can be obtained from underground and nearby are the docks of the Humber ports for the export of the finished products.

44 *A quick-freezing plant at Grimsby*

Work to do

1. Using an atlas make a map to show the rivers which drain into the North Sea through the Humber estuary.
2. From the plan (Fig 39) make a simple sketch map of Goole Docks. On it mark and name: the River Ouse; the locks; the transit sheds; the coaling appliances; the railway sidings; an arrow to show the direction of north.
3. From an atlas make an outline map of the countries which border the North Sea. On it mark and name the ports which have regular sailings to and from Goole. Put an arrow from each of these to Goole; add a title.
4. Draw a map of the Humber estuary and show on it the four main ports. Beside each port, make a short note about its trade.
5. If your school has copies of earlier editions of this book, make a table to show how the trade and activities of the Humber ports have changed in recent years. Try to explain the changes you have identified.
6. Look for a diagram of a modern stern trawler, and how a canal lock works. Make annotated copies in your exercise book.
7. Considerable changes are being made to the road transport network of Humberside. Using a source book such as the AA handbook make a map to show the road network of Humberside before the changes took place and another map to show the network once the new roads have been completed. How will these changes affect (i) the county of Humberside as a whole (ii) access to and from the Humberside ports?
8. Discuss possible solutions to the problems caused on Humberside by the fishing limits imposed around Iceland.

6 | SCUNTHORPE AND NORTH LINCOLNSHIRE

45 *An iron ore quarry, near Scunthorpe.*

Iron Ore Mining near Scunthorpe

The photograph (Fig. 45) shows work in progress at a quarry near Scunthorpe in South Humberside in part of the Frodingham ore field. A machine is used, in the area shown in the foreground, to drill a series of holes, about one and a half metres (five feet) apart, into a hard bed of ironstone. These are carefully charged with explosives which are detonated electrically. The blast shatters the rock and it can then be loaded into dump trucks by a mechanical shovel as can be seen in the centre of the picture. In the distance an excavator is being used to remove about fifteen metres (fifty feet) of clay, called the overburden, to uncover the iron ore. Once this has been extracted bulldozers set to work restoring the land for agriculture.

The map on the following page (Map C) shows that there are a number of quarries in this part of Lincolnshire. Notice that they are found on the low ground which runs from north to south between two ridges of higher land. One problem facing the miners is the way the overburden thickens towards the east. Eventually the ore becomes too deep to be worked by opencast methods and underground mining becomes necessary, as near Dragonby (903141). This is because the rocks which contain the seams of ore dip towards the east. They belong to the Jurassic series from which iron ore was once mined in the Cleveland Hills.

Single track railways link the quarries, like the one in the photograph, with the steelworks in Scunthorpe. In 1976 the Appleby/Frodingham works (Map C) on the east of the town was amalgamated with the smaller Normanby Park steel works to the north of Scunthorpe, marked at grid reference 889137 on Map C, to form the British Steel Corporation's Scunthorpe Works which operates the quarries, underground mine and the two steelworks under one board of management.

49

Map C *Based on part of OS Sheet 112*

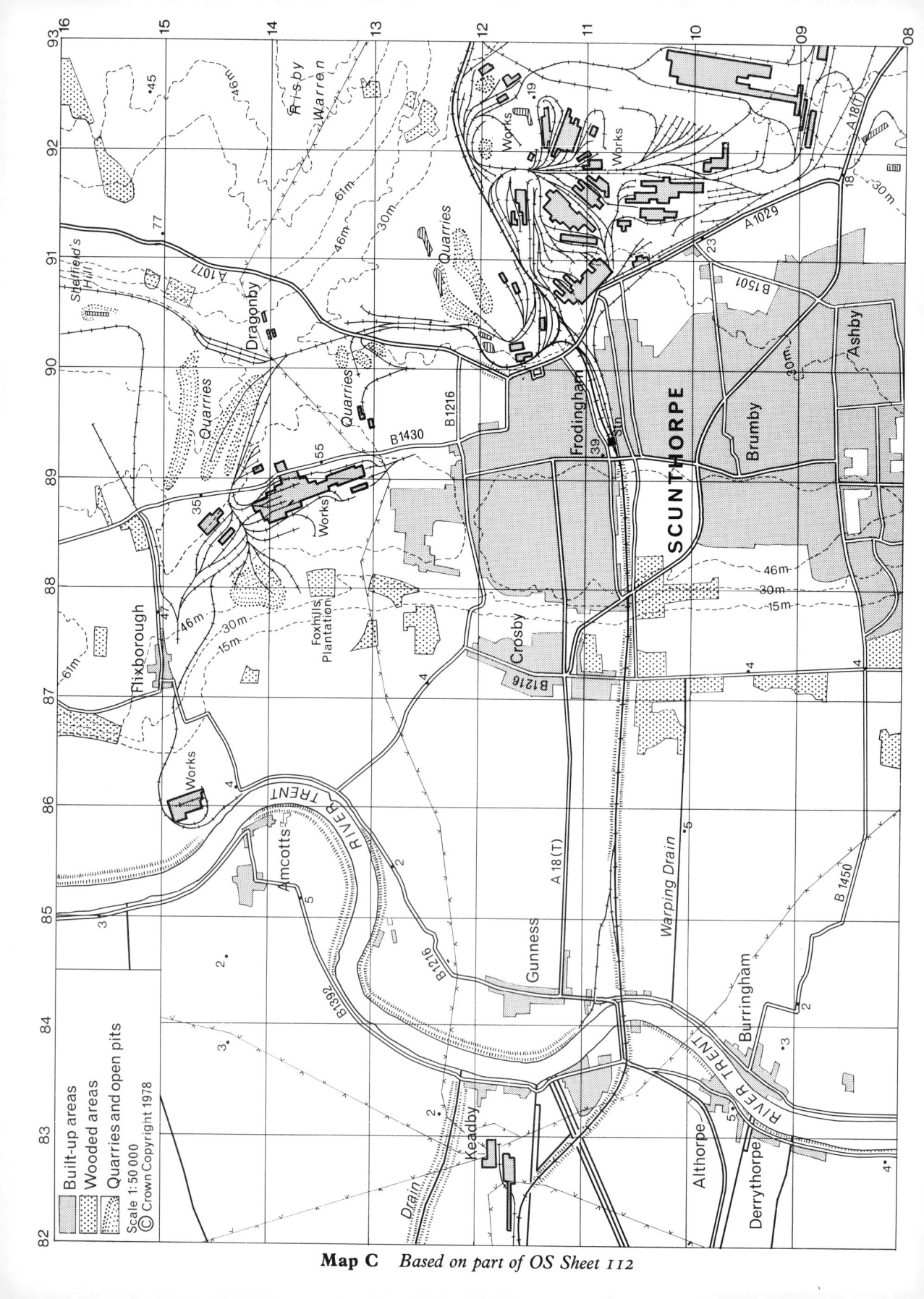

Making Steel in Scunthorpe

The diagram (Fig 46) shows what happens to the iron ore when it arrives at the steelworks. First it is crushed, then blended with other additives before being despatched to an ore blending plant. The Lincolnshire ores are said to be 'lean' because they have an iron content of only 23 per cent. For this reason they are blended with high grade foreign ore. This is imported through an ore terminal on the Humber at Immingham which serves all the Scunthorpe works. The blending is done at Frodingham and the ore is then sent by conveyor systems to the preparation plants.

Here it is mixed with coke and heated in a process called sintering which burns off some of the impurities. The sinter is fed into the blast furnaces together with coke. About $2\frac{1}{2}$ million tonnes of coke a year are made from coal at the works' coke ovens. About eighty per cent of the coal is from pits in the Yorkshire and Nottinghamshire Coalfields. It is brought by rail, on the merry-go-round system, along the line which crosses the Trent at Keadby Bridge (841 107) and it arrives at a central handling plant in Dawes Lane.

The purpose of a blast furnace is to remove oxygen and other impurities from the iron. It consists of a vertical steel cylinder lined with firebricks. A hot blast of air causes the coke to burn fiercely at the bottom of the furnace. The iron melts in the heat and is tapped at the bottom of the furnace at intervals of three to four hours. The Lincolnshire iron ores contain over twenty per cent lime which acts as a flux by mixing together with the other impurities to form slag. This floats on top of the molten iron and is drained off periodically.

While still molten the iron is taken in huge

46 *Making steel in Scunthorpe. Works flow chart 1978.*

WORKS FLOW CHART 1978
(Outputs in million tonnes per annum)

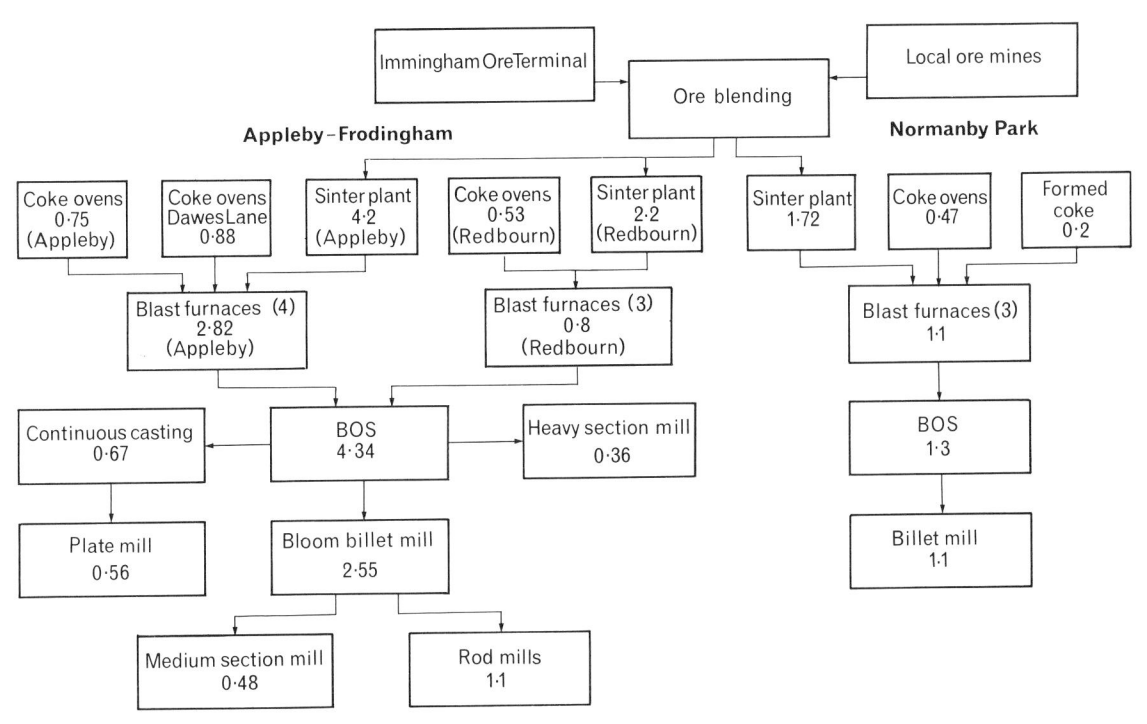

```
                          Immingham Ore Terminal → Ore blending ← Local ore mines

        Appleby-Frodingham                                         Normanby Park

Coke ovens   Coke ovens    Sinter plant   Coke ovens    Sinter plant    Sinter plant   Coke ovens    Formed
0.75         Dawes Lane    4.2            0.53          2.2             1.72           0.47          coke
(Appleby)    0.88          (Appleby)      (Redbourn)    (Redbourn)                                   0.2

        Blast furnaces (4)              Blast furnaces (3)              Blast furnaces (3)
        2.82                            0.8                             1.1
        (Appleby)                       (Redbourn)

Continuous casting    BOS          Heavy section mill                    BOS
0.67                  4.34         0.36                                  1.3

Plate mill            Bloom billet mill                                  Billet mill
0.56                  2.55                                               1.1

            Medium section mill    Rod mills
            0.48                   1.1
```

51

vessels called torpedos, which hold up to 250 tonnes of 'hot metal', to be converted into steel. There are two steelmaking plants at the Scunthorpe Works where steel is made by the Basic Oxygen System (BOS). At the Normanby Park Steelworks there are three interchangeable vessels, two being in use at any one time, making up to 85 tonnes of steel every 40 minutes. At the Appleby/Frodingham works, which was commissioned in 1973 as part of the Anchor Scheme, about 300 tonnes of steel is made every 40 minutes. The purpose of the BOS process is to burn out the impurities from the iron by oxygen injection and thus convert it into steel.

The molten steel is either poured into ladles and then into ingot moulds or sent to a continuous casting plant to be cast into 'blooms' which are then cast into plates. When the steel which has been cast into moulds has cooled the moulds are stripped off and the ingots, each weighing up to 14 tonnes, are taken to the soaking pits. Here they are kept heated with gas from the blast furnaces and coke ovens. Finally the ingots are rolled out to form bars and rods of various sizes. The annual output of the Scunthorpe Works is $5\frac{1}{2}$ million tonnes a year which represents a fifth of Britain's total steel production.

The Growth of Scunthorpe

Visitors to Scunthorpe soon notice that it is a modern town with few old buildings. This is because most of it has been built since 1900 with the development of the steel industry. Just over a hundred years ago, when iron ores were first exploited in the district, Scunthorpe was a small hamlet lying close to the village of Frodingham. In those days the ore was sent for smelting to the Yorkshire Coalfield near Barnsley. Blast furnaces were soon built at Scunthorpe because the low iron content in the ore and new ways of using coal more effectively made it cheaper to bring the fuel from Yorkshire to the ironfield than to take iron ore to the coalfield.

By 1890, when the first steel was made in this area, Frodingham and Scunthorpe had merged into one and had a population of about 3,000. Now there are 67,400 people living in the town and the steelworks employ 13,500. Other industries in the town such as the making of fertilisers and tar, and engineering, all depend on the steelworks for their raw materials. Clothing and footwear manufacturers provide jobs for women in the area.

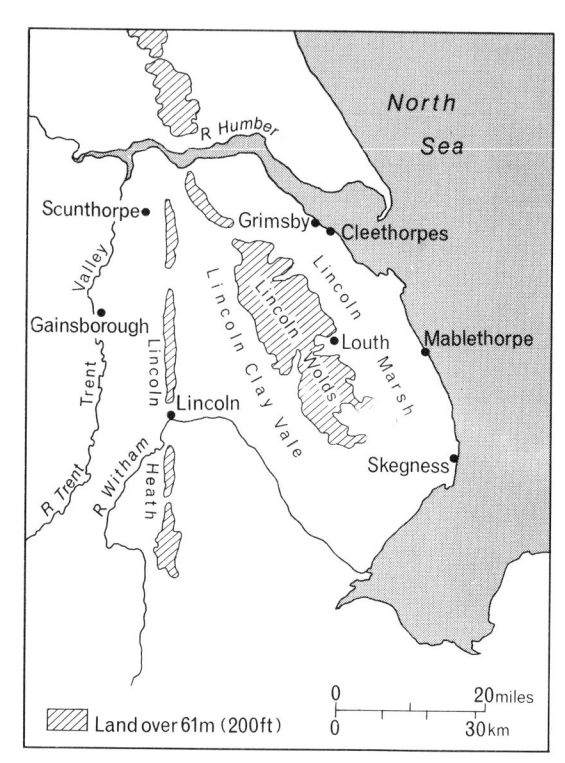

47 *The relief of North Lincolnshire and Humberside*

The Scarplands and Vales of North Lincolnshire

The geology section A–B in Chapter 1 (Fig 4) shows that the rocks of North Lincolnshire are tilted towards the east. The more resistant Jurassic limestone and chalk give rise to the west-facing escarpments of Lincoln Heath and the Wolds (Fig 47). The less resistant rocks, chiefly clays, have been eroded to form the lowlands of the Vale of Trent, Lincoln Clay Vale and Lincoln Marsh. To the south the Clay Vale broadens out and merges into the Fens.

Some of Britain's richest farmland is found in North Lincolnshire where more than 60 per cent of the total area is arable. Barley and wheat are grown on over a half of the cultivated land and potatoes, sugar beet and vegetables are also important. Farming in this part of

England has not always been arable; two hundred years ago it was noted for its livestock and rich pastures. The changes are the result of improvements in farming similar to those made in Yorkshire and described in Chapters 2 and 3.

The Trent Valley. The spot heights on the map of Scunthorpe (Map C, p. 50) show that the Trent is bordered with low-lying land. The straight embanked courses of the tributary rivers, the large number of drainage ditches and the warping drain at grid reference 857102, indicate that the area is warpland. It is part of the land south of the Humber drained by Vermuyden in the seventeenth century and later improved by warping. How this was done and the type of land use found there, are explained in Chapter 2.

The Clay Vale and the Marsh. The cultivated area in the Clay Vale and the Marsh has also been increased by drainage and reclamation. In the north of the Clay Vale a new channel for the River Ancholme was cut in 1637 to prevent flooding. Today the reclaimed parts of both the Vale and the Marsh are used for growing cash crops. The cultivation of sugar beet is particularly important and there are sugar factories at Brigg and Bardney. In summer much of the pastureland is rented to farmers from the Wolds for grazing sheep.

The Heath. Whereas the Clay lands must be artificially drained to grow good crops, the Heath and the Wolds are naturally well-drained because their underlying rocks are permeable. The Heath is the upland area which lies to the east of Scunthorpe, marked on Map C (p. 50). Although its maximum height is only 76.5 metres (251 feet) (912150) the Heath forms the highest part of the map. Notice the steep scarp on its western side at Sheffield's Hill (909158). This is such a prominent feature that the Heath escarpment is sometimes called the Cliff, or Edge.

The name of the Heath dates from the time when it was an area of rough grazing suitable only for sheep. During the last century improvements in farming like those in the Wolds brought many parts of the area under cultivation. Barley, wheat and roots are the main crops though large numbers of sheep are still reared. Risby Warren (931138) is one area of rough grazing which has not been improved. Here the limestone is covered with infertile sands blown from the Vale of Trent by the wind. Notice that small parts of it have been planted with coniferous trees; similar areas to the south have undergone more extensive afforestation. Villages occur along the edges of the Heath, frequently where springs emerge at the junction of the limestone and the clays.

The Wolds. The chalk rocks of the Wolds rise to over 150 metres (500 feet) and form an escarpment which slopes steeply to the Clay Vale in the west and gently to the Marsh in the east. Like the Wolds of Yorkshire they were once covered with open grasslands which were used for grazing sheep. Now over 70 per cent of the land is ploughed for crops of barley, wheat, clover and roots. Livestock are still important and large numbers of both sheep and cattle are reared. As in the Yorkshire Wolds, the changes came in the nineteenth century with the adoption of a more scientific system of farming.

The Coast of North Lincolnshire

Five kilometres (three miles) from Skegness on the Lincolnshire coast is one of Butlin's Holiday Camps. Its many amenities include two swimming pools, a boating lake, an amusement park, four ballrooms, a miniature railway and a monorail. It is in fact a complete holiday village with chalets, shops, restaurants, a Post Office and even Launderettes, all set in acres of landscaped grounds. The holidaymakers can also enjoy the warm dry summers, sandy beaches and bracing sea air of the Lincolnshire coast.

Skegness (13,590), Cleethorpes (38,000) and Mablethorpe (6,956) are holiday resorts which attract large numbers of visitors from all over Britain, but mainly from Yorkshire and the Midlands. Their growth began in the nineteenth century with the building of railways but has been increased by motor transport.

The scenery of the coast, like that of Holderness, is low and flat. Near Mablethorpe erosion by the waves is so active that the shore has retreated eight hundred metres (half a mile) inland in the last 400 years. Elsewhere sand from the beach has been heaped up by the wind to form dunes. These are up to twelve metres (forty feet) high and protect the lowlying areas inland from the high tides of the North Sea. Longshore drifting carries beach material south down the coast to Gibraltar Point where a spit has been formed.

48 *Lincoln Cathedral*

Lincoln (73,100)

The photograph (Fig 48) shows Lincoln Cathedral from the north west. The cathedral stands on an elevated site overlooking the centre of the town. From its high central tower it is possible on a clear day to see as far as Boston, nearly forty-five kilometres (thirty miles) away in the fens of south Lincolnshire. It was built in the Middle Ages, with limestone quarried out of Lincoln Heath, to replace an earlier Norman church which had been damaged by an earthquake.

To the west of the cathedral is Lincoln Castle which also dates from the Middle Ages. Both the Cathedral and the Castle are found in the oldest part of the city on the high ground which lies to the north of the gap cut by the River Witham through Lincoln Heath (Fig 49). The advantages of the site were recognised by the Romans who built a fort there which they called 'Lindum'. Later, as at York, a civilian town grew up which became one of the most important in Britain.

The map (Fig 49) shows that the Romans built a system of roads to converge on Lincoln. One of

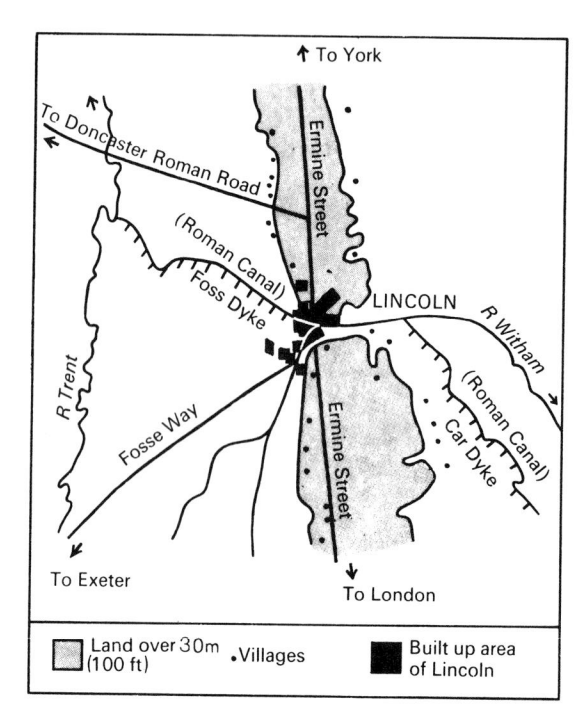

49 *The position of Lincoln*

them, Ermine Street, runs in a straight line along Lincoln Heath. In Roman times the Heath was lightly wooded and thus offered an easier route than the forested lowlands to the east and west. It was the Romans who first cut the canal, Foss Dyke, to link the Trent with the Witham which flows south-east to the Wash. They also drained parts of the Fens to grow the crops of grain needed to feed their legions at York and along Hadrian's Wall.

When the Roman occupation of Britain ended, the Saxons invaded Lincolnshire and set up a kingdom in the north called 'Lindsey'. They were followed by the Danes who divided the county into three parts which became known as Lindsey, Holland and Kesteven. Until 1974 these old divisions were used in the local government of Lincolnshire in a similar way to the Ridings of Yorkshire.

The coming of the Normans brought great changes to Lincoln because William the Conqueror ordered a castle and a cathedral to be built in the city. In the period which followed Lincoln prospered through the export of wool from Lincolnshire and the Midlands to Flanders. By the end of the fourteenth century Lincoln had lost its wool trade to Boston and the city declined in importance. It was not until the draining of the Fens and the improvement of farming on the Wolds that Lincoln's fortunes were revived. The city then became a market town for the rich farmlands of Lincolnshire. The opening of the railway from Nottingham in 1846 led to the growth of industry and a rise in population.

The photograph (Fig 50) was taken in one of the heavy machine shops at the Lincoln works of Ruston-Bucyrus. It shows various components being machined for use in the manufacture of

50 *Ruston-Bucyrus Works, Lincoln*

excavators. Rustons, who employ about 2,000 people, make lifting cranes and marine cranes as well as an extensive range of excavators. Their equipment is used in the iron ore quarries of Lincolnshire and much of it is exported. The works are typical of the industries now found in Lincoln where engineering employs over a third of the city's workers. The products of the engineering industry include mining machinery, diesel engines, gas turbines and machinery for pumping and drilling. Among the other industries in Lincoln are the making of plastics, electrical components, clothing, paper, potato crisps and animal feed stuffs.

Work to do

1. Sketch a relief section from west to east across Map C from 820140 to 930160. On it mark and name (a) the River Trent; (b) the scarp slopes at 868148 and Sheffield's Hill (907156); (c) any evidence of opencast mining. Add a title.
2. The large buildings at 828117 on Map C are part of Keadby Power Station. Refer to Chapter 8 and then suggest reasons why a power station was built here.
3. (a) Try to find out more about the Anchor Project at Scunthorpe.
   (b) Teesside, South Wales and Clydeside are areas in Britain where the steel industry is to be expanded. What factors have they in common with Scunthorpe? In what ways are they different?
   (c) Choose one area where the steel industry is declining. What are the reasons for its decline? What will the consequences be for the area?
4. The population of Scunthorpe and important events in its growth.

Date	Population	Event
1864	Under 3,000	First blast furnace
1890	3,000	First steel made
1900	4,000	
1916		Rebuilding of Keadby road and rail bridge
1931	34,000	
1936		Made a Municipal Borough
1951	54,000	
1954		Building of the biggest blast furnace in Europe
1961	67,527	
1967	71,010	
1971	70,880	
1978	67,400	

   Make a line graph to show the growth of population in Scunthorpe since 1864. Add notes to show the important events in its growth and suggest reasons why the population has declined since 1967. Compare this with the graph for Middlesbrough in Chapter 7. Make a similar graph for your local town.
5. The words 'by' or 'thorpe' at the end of a place-name show that the settlement was probably formed by the Danes. Make a survey of the place-names on Map C and construct a graph from the results to show the number of Danish and other place-names.

7 | TEESSIDE

Bridges Across the River Tees

The Transporter Bridge (Fig 51) links Port Clarence on the north bank of the River Tees with the old centre of Middlesbrough on the south. It is the nearest bridge to the sea across the Tees. The Transporter carries vehicles and passengers over the river in a 'car' suspended by wires from an iron superstructure. It saves travellers a journey of several miles because the next bridge is three kilometres (two miles) upstream at Newport. This bridge has a centre section which can be raised like a giant lift from towers on opposite banks of the river. The Newport and Transporter bridges allow vessels to sail upriver to the wharves which line the Tees as far as Thornaby and Stockton although there is now little commercial shipping upstream of the Transporter Bridge. A stone and iron bridge, first built in 1769, links Stockton and Thornaby. This bridge and the shallowness of the water prevent all but small craft sailing further upstream. A new road bridge now spans the river upstream

51 *The Transporter Bridge and Old Middlesbrough from the south*

Key
A To Docks   B To Ironmasters' District   C Parish Church   D Old town hall

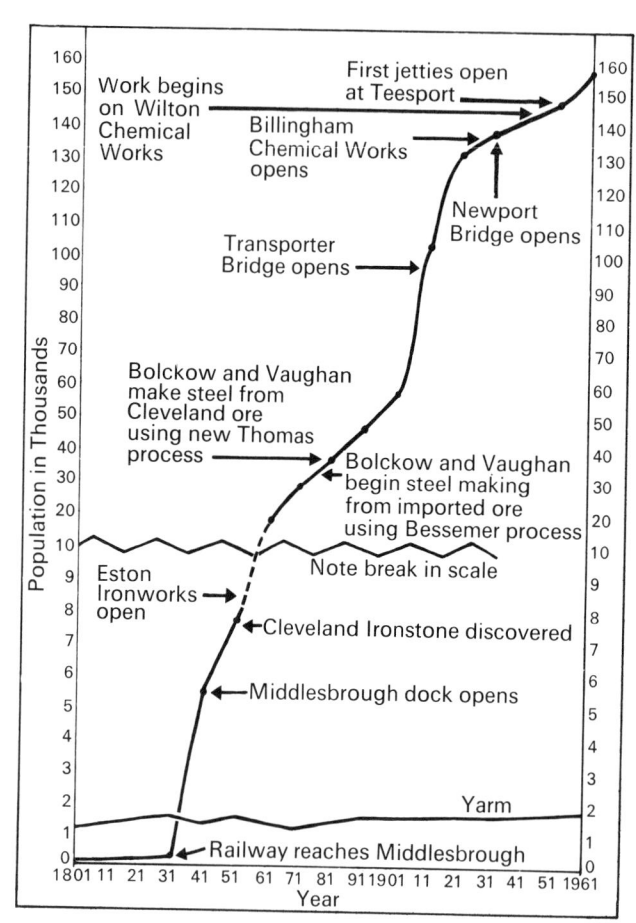

52 *Population graphs for Middlesbrough and Yarm showing some of the events which affected the growth of population on Teesside*

from Newport. It carries the re-routed A19 which allows traffic bound for Tyne and Wear to by-pass the Teesside towns.

In the Middle Ages, many ships sailed as far as Yarm, ten kilometres (six miles) upriver from Stockton. Yarm was then the chief port and lowest bridging point on the Tees with shipbuilding and textile industries. Even as late as 1801 it had a population many times greater than Middlesbrough which was a hamlet with only twenty five inhabitants.

The Growth of Middlesbrough

Fig 51 shows the old centre of Middlesbrough in the foreground. Notice the rectangular plan of the streets with the parish church, market place and old town hall at the centre. Until recently the streets were lined with old terraced houses like those on the left of the photograph. Many have now been demolished and replaced by more modern houses and flats. Notice the cargo boats lining the riverside wharves. Railway sidings serve each wharf.

The railway reached Middlesbrough in 1831, only six years after the opening of the Stockton to Darlington Railway. This famous line, the first in the United Kingdom, was built to carry coal from the southern part of the Durham coalfield to Stockton for export. There was so much traffic that it was decided to extend the railway down to deeper water nearer the mouth of the Tees. The site shown in the photograph was chosen as the new terminus. At the wharves coal was loaded into ships which carried it to London. Shortly after the building of the railway, the little town, with its rectangular plan, was laid out. By 1842 a large dock had been constructed just to the east of the town. Iron works were built near to the dock and to the west in what became known as the Ironmasters' District. Here iron ore and pig iron could be imported and coking coal brought in by rail from the Durham coalfield.

The growth of the port and industries caused the population to increase rapidly as people came seeking work. The graph (Fig 52) shows that by 1851, Middlesbrough was many times larger than Yarm. By 1961 its population was 157,000. Yarm, further up river and prevented by a shallow channel and by bridges from becoming a modern port, has hardly changed in size since 1801. Notice on the graph the various events which have been responsible for the growth of Middlesbrough and the nearby towns. In April 1974 seven large towns bordering the Tees, Middlesbrough, Thornaby, Eston, Redcar, Billingham, Stockton, and Hartlepool, along with some neighbouring rural and smaller urban areas merged to form the new Cleveland County with a population of 565,000. The increases in population over the last 100 years have been brought about by the growth of industries, especially steel and chemicals, along the banks of the Tees.

The Iron and Steel Industry of Teesside

The North East of England is Britain's second largest steel making district. In 1965 it produced 4,800,000 tonnes of steel, mostly in works alongside the River Tees. The larger ones are like the steelworks at Scunthorpe described in Chapter 6. They smelt iron ore in blast furnaces, convert the iron into steel and then roll it into bars, plates, sheets, girders, wire and many other shapes.

In the photograph of British Steel's Cleveland Works (Fig 53), notice the three tall blast furnaces, the gas holder, and the railways and overhead conveyors which keep the furnaces supplied with ore and coke. The sloping metal framework on the left of each furnace is known as a skip hoist. It lifts iron ore, coke and limestone to the top of the vertical cylinder which is the main part of the furnace. Into the base of this cylinder is forced a blast of hot air which causes the coke to burn fiercely and separate the iron from the impurities in the ore. Molten iron sinks to the bottom of the furnace from where it is 'tapped' through a small hole. The pipes at the top of the furnaces collect the gases produced during smelting. These can be used for heating the air blast, raising steam, heating steel furnaces and firing the coke ovens.

The furnaces are 'charged' with high quality ore imported from places such as Sweden, Labrador, and Mauritania. For many years however, ironstone mines in the Cleveland and Eston Hills, a few miles south of the Tees were an important source of ore. In 1850, John Vaughan, a local iron manufacturer, discovered a five metre (sixteen foot) thick seam of ironstone in the Eston Hills only ten kilometres (six miles) from Middlesbrough. He and his partner, Henry Bolckow built a railway to carry ore from their mines at Eston to their ironworks near Middlesbrough Dock. In 1854 they opened a new works where their private railway joined the Middlesbrough–Redcar line, the site of the present Cleveland Works (Fig 54). Many more mines and ironworks opened in the years that followed. By 1875, more

53 *Blast furnaces at the Cleveland Works of the British Steel Corporation*

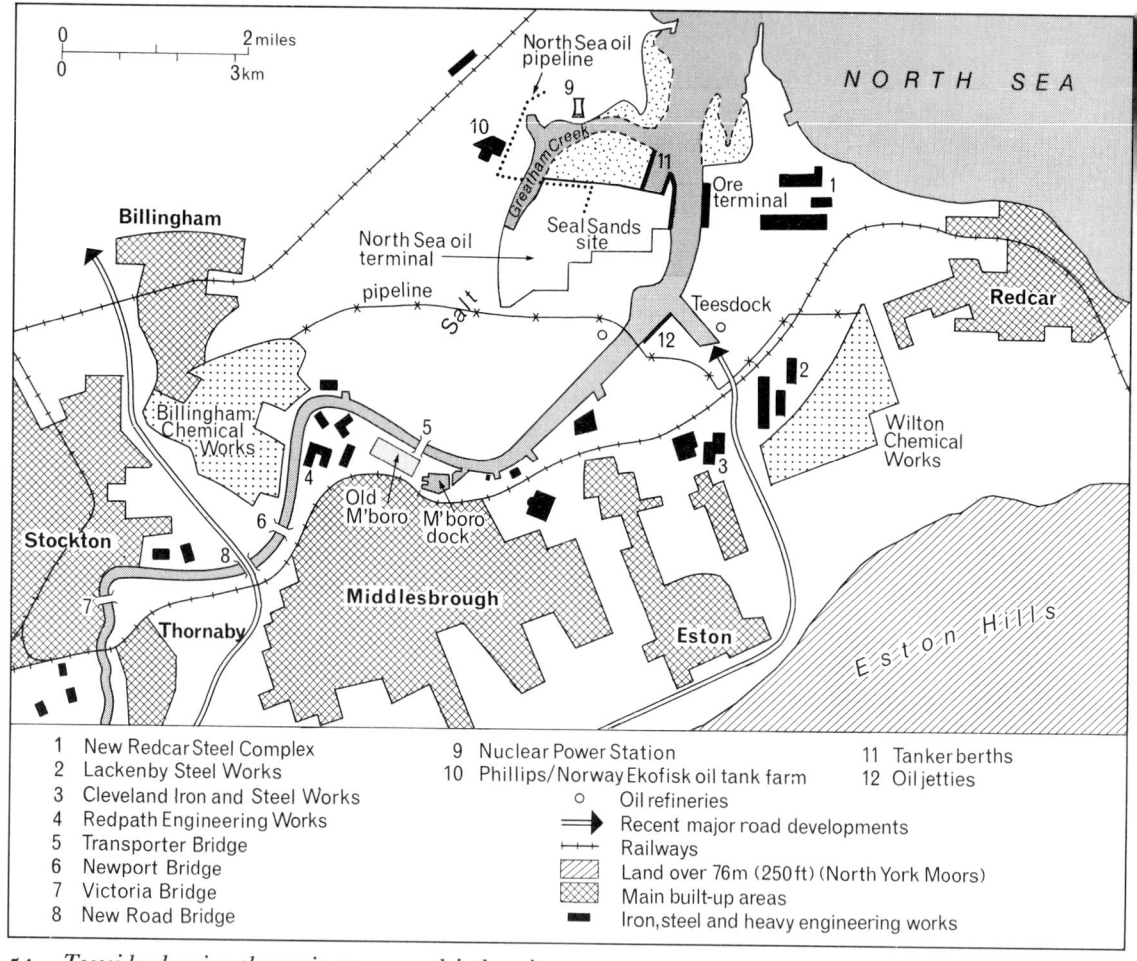

54 *Teesside showing the main towns and industries*

Key:
1. New Redcar Steel Complex
2. Lackenby Steel Works
3. Cleveland Iron and Steel Works
4. Redpath Engineering Works
5. Transporter Bridge
6. Newport Bridge
7. Victoria Bridge
8. New Road Bridge
9. Nuclear Power Station
10. Phillips/Norway Ekofisk oil tank farm
11. Tanker berths
12. Oil jetties

○ Oil refineries
⇒ Recent major road developments
Railways
Land over 76m (250 ft) (North York Moors)
Main built-up areas
Iron, steel and heavy engineering works

than six million tonnes of ore and one and a quarter million tonnes of iron were being produced annually. Much of the iron was used for making railway lines and ships. Later in the century, steel making was introduced using both Cleveland and imported iron ores. Today the iron ore used in the Teesside steel industry is wholly imported. The last Cleveland mine to produce ore, at North Skelton, closed in 1964.

Fig 54 shows the position of Lackenby steel works and how well placed it is to obtain iron ore from overseas. It is next to the river where the British Steel Corporation has built a terminal for ships bringing ore from abroad. Nearby there is another terminal for exporting finished steel. A short distance away to the north is the Durham Coalfield which supplies good coking coal. Limestone is obtained from quarries in the Pennines.

The oldest works are crowded together in the Ironmasters' District. They now concentrate on heavy engineering rather than iron smelting. One of them is the Teesside Engineering Works of Redpath, whose predecessor Dorman Long built many famous bridges such as the Sydney Harbour Bridge. The works further east have been built more recently on large open sites partly reclaimed from tidal marshes. The newest steel works is British Steel's Lackenby Works opened in 1965. Fig 55 shows the coil plate mill at these Works. Ingots from the steel furnaces enter the mill building where they pass through rollers like the one in the photograph. Gradually the hot metal is squeezed into plates or other shapes such as girders, rods, bars and rails. The whole process is automated and is controlled from a 'pulpit', seen on the left of Fig. 55. Computers check the progress of the steel through the mill and feed information back to the operator. The Lackenby Works are linked by a private railway to a new blast furnace at Redcar, which supplies iron to it for steel-making. The Lackenby and other Teesside works make large amounts of structural steel for such things as bridges, high buildings, power stations and oil refineries. At Redcar the British Steel Corporation has already built an ore terminal, coke ovens, sinter plant and pellet plant. A new 10,000 tonne a day blast furnace was opened in 1979, completing a £400m iron-making development scheme.

The Wilton Works of Imperial Chemical Industries Ltd

Before 1946, the area shown in Fig 56 was quiet farmland at Wilton Grange Farm between Eston and Redcar. I.C.I. have since built a large chemical plant on the 809 hectare (2,000 acre) site which employs about 13,000 people. It stands on flat land between the River Tees to the north and the Cleveland Hills to the south. The factories are linked by pipelines which pass through two tunnels under the river to the huge I.C.I. Billingham complex, ten kilometres (six miles) away on the north bank. The Billingham factory of I.C.I.'s Agricultural Division can manufac-

55 *Coil plate mill at Lackenby Steelworks*

56 *ICI Wilton Chemical Works*

ture very large quantities of ammonia, methanol and carbon dioxide. Other important activities include producing fertilisers and other agricultural chemicals as well as the development of new chemical processes such as the manufacture of urea. One reason why Wilton was chosen as the site for a chemical works was its nearness to Billingham which could supply some of its raw materials. The choice was also influenced by the good rail, road and sea communications in the area as well as by the supply of labour. The main chemical used at Wilton is naphtha which is refined from crude oil. Tankers bring the naphtha to jetties from where it is pumped to the works. Numerous pipelines carry chemicals to and fro between different parts of the works. The most important products are olefines which are used in the manufacture of a wide variety of synthetic fibres and plastics at Wilton.

Teesport

In 1830, Middlesbrough began to grow as a coal shipping port. Since 1946, wharves and a new dock have been built at Teesport, five kilometres (three miles) downstream from the Middlesbrough Dock. Developments are taking place around the new port much as they did around the older one in the nineteenth century.

The aerial photograph of Teesport (Fig. 57), shows Tees Dock and some of the industrial development which has taken place near to it. The layout of the Lackenby Steel Works can be seen clearly from the photograph. On the left are the chimneys of the steel furnaces. The long buildings are the rolling mills. There are rails beside each mill along which overhead cranes carry the rolled steel to await despatch to customers.

Tankers of up to 200 metres (650 feet) in length can discharge their cargoes at the oil

57 *An aerial view of the Teesport area from the south*

Key

A Construction yard for oil production platforms
B Nuclear power station
C Redcar ore terminal
D Redcar steel complex
E Seal Sands
F Steel export terminal
G Tees Dock
H Potash terminal
I Container terminal
J Shell refinery
K Roll-on/roll-off terminals
L Lackenby steel works

jetties where products from oil refineries are piped ashore. Naphtha goes straight to the Wilton Works. From the 'tank farms', petrol and fuel oil are distributed to factories and garages. Because of the demand for petrol, oil and petrochemicals from industry and transport, two large oil refineries have been built. The Shell and I.C.I. oil refineries import about 7·7 million tonnes of oil a year, about 1·2 million tonnes of which comes by ship from the North Sea. A further 13 million tonnes a year is landed by pipeline at Seal Sands from the Ekofisk field in the North Sea. About 2 million tonnes of this is used locally; the rest is exported by sea.

The Tees Dock has five general cargo berths and two specialised steel berths. Cranes, transit sheds, and open storage areas line the berths.

The Greatham and Seal Sands North Sea Oil Terminal

This is one of Teesside's most important new industrial developments. In 1975 the 220 mile pipeline connecting the Ekofisk North Sea oil field to the oil terminal at Seal Sands was opened. The Phillips Norway Group (a consortium of oil companies) own the terminal which has been constructed on two adjacent sites (see Fig 54). The 202 hectare (500 acre) site at Seal Sands is land reclaimed from the surrounding tidal area by a two year dredging operation. It includes an eight-berth jetty designed for very large tankers.

The crude oil is pumped ashore at Seal Sands and the natural gas liquids are separated out. The crude oil can then be stored and it is pumped along a pipeline buried under Greatham Creek to the oil tank farm on the 160 hectare (400 acre) Greatham Site. Here there are ten oil storage tanks which can hold up to ¾ million barrels of crude oil.

Crude oil and liquefied petroleum gas are both exported from the Seal Sands jetty in tankers of up to 150,000 tonnes. Since its completion in 1977, the terminal has increased its capacity

58 *Tesside in 1830 and 1970*

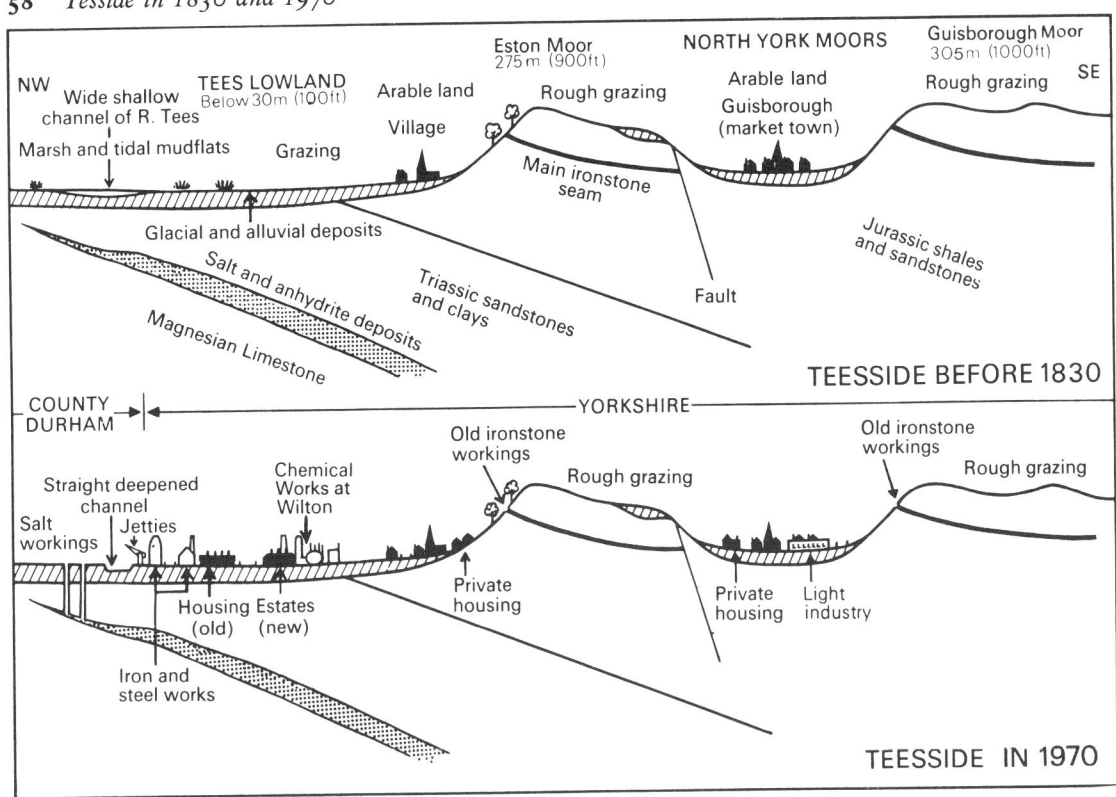

to around one million barrels of crude oil and natural gas liquids a day.

The many changes described in this chapter have taken place since 1830. Before that, Teesside was a quiet, rural area. Now towns, industries, docks, roads and railways line the river and are quickly engulfing the countryside. Fig 58 summarises the changes which took place up to 1970. Why has all this happened in 140 years? Some of the answers have been given in this chapter: (i) the nearness of Teesside to the South Durham Coalfield; (ii) the early development of railways; (iii) local raw materials, especially iron ore and salt which helped the growth of large iron and steel and chemical industries; (iv) the mouth of the River Tees has enabled a large port to be built which can import raw materials and export manufactured goods cheaply by water; (v) reclaimed tidal flats have provided suitable industrial building land.

Many other developments have taken place at the mouth of the Tees. These include a potash terminal at Teesport for the Boulby Mine (see Chapter 3), the steelworks at Redcar, and a nuclear power station on the north bank (see Figs 54 and 58). To the south, however, the North Yorkshire National Park remains relatively unchanged. It attracts many visitors from the industrial counties of Cleveland, West and South Yorkshire.

Work to do

1. Explain briefly:
   (a) why iron and steel works were built near to Middlesbrough after 1850;
   (b) why the steel and chemical works are now located close to the mouth of the Tees.
2. Find out how the following types of steel furnace work: the Bessemer converter; the open hearth furnace; the electric arc furnace; the basic oxygen converter.
3. After reading chapters 6 and 9, make a list of differences between the steel industries of Teesside, Scunthorpe, and Sheffield.
4. Study reference books, pamphlets and wall charts dealing with the oil industry. Make notes and diagrams or mount a wall display using the headings set out below.
   (a) The sources of Britain's crude oil.
   (b) Where oil refineries are located in Britain.
   (c) Oil and gas discoveries in the North Sea.
   (d) The effects of North Sea oil.
   (e) How petrol and fuel oils reach the customer.
5. Draw a sketch map of the area shown in Fig 57. Label the features named and any others you can identify.
6. Study Fig. 58 which shows Teesside in 1830 and 1970. Draw a similar diagram to illustrate the situation in the early 1980s making use of the up-to-date information in this chapter.
7. Prepare on A4 paper a publicity brochure advertising the advantages of the new county of Cleveland for the location of industry.
8. Write an essay on the changing economic geography of Teesside using Fig. 58 and the diagram you drew in exercise 6.

8 | THE YORKSHIRE COALFIELD

Kellingley Colliery

The coal miner in the photograph (Fig 59) is operating a coal 'shearer' at Kellingley Colliery near Knottingley in the Yorkshire Coalfield. The colliery is one of the newest in the country. Both at the surface and underground it has many up-to-date features. At one of the coal faces in the Beeston seam, which is almost three metres (nine and a half feet) thick, the shearer moves to and fro along a 183 metre (two hundred yard) face taking off a slice of coal nearly two metres (seven feet) high. It leaves about two thirds of a metre (two feet) of coal to form a clean solid roof. Behind the slicer the roof is held up by hydraulic supports seen on the left of the picture. These move forward at the touch of a lever allowing the roof to cave in behind. The coal is automatically loaded on to a network of conveyors which carry it to the bottom of the shaft. There it is transferred into large 'skips' to be wound to the surface. A large underground cavern 137 metres (150 yds) long and 6.7 metres (22 feet) high has been excavated to store coal at times of peak production. All of the mining operations are monitored by remote-control electronic equipment so that the colliery manager is able to see the working of the whole pit on a control panel in the office building at the surface.

The aerial view (Fig 60) shows the surface buildings at Kellingley. All collieries have a similar layout although they may not be as up-to-date. Notice the two shafts which are essential for safety and ventilation. If one shaft was damaged, the miners could escape up the other. Huge fans ventilate the pit by drawing foul air up one shaft and sucking fresh air down the other. Each shaft has a set of winding gear, driven by electricity. One hauls coal from the shaft bottom, the other carries men and materials.

At the surface, the coal is conveyed from the

59 *A coal 'shearer' at work in the Beeston Seam at Kellingley Colliery*

Key
A Shafts and winding gear
B Workshops
C Fan house
D Coal preparation plant
E Railway sidings
F Baths
G Offices
H Canteen

60 *Kellingley Colliery from the air*

pithead to the coal preparation plant where it is washed to remove stones and other material which will not burn. Conveyors then carry it to the screens which work rather like a garden riddle and sort the coal into different sizes. It is then despatched to the customer by rail, road and canal. Notice from the photograph (Fig 60) how well the colliery is served by communications. The road in the foreground is the A645 which linked Goole and Hull to West Yorkshire before the M62 opened; to the right is the Knottingley–Goole railway and at the top right just beyond the photograph is the Aire and Calder canal. These facilities enable the coal to be transported easily and quickly away from the colliery after it has been washed and graded.

The buildings to the left of Fig 60 include baths, a canteen, the lamproom, a medical centre and offices. Notice the well-kept lawns and the trees which screen the colliery from the road. There is no unsightly tip of waste material like those which disfigure the older, western parts of the coalfield. The waste is taken by lorry to fill in old quarries and low-lying marshland at nearby Gale Common.

Eventually, Kellingley will produce 40,000 tonnes of coal a week and as there are 200 million tonnes in the 'take', which is more than six kilometres (four miles) square, the colliery should have a life of over 100 years. These figures were all worked out before building began at Kellingley since the National Coal Board had to be certain that there would be enough coal to make it worth spending the £15/16 million it cost to build. Many boreholes were drilled to find the thickness, depth and number of seams inside the take from which the amount of coal present was worked out. Fig 61 shows the seams found in the shaft. Note that the coal-bearing rocks are buried beneath nearly 152 metres (500 feet) of limestone. The seams, especially the Beeston, are of a good thickness and quality and in spite of their depth have repaid the construction costs. Work began on sinking the shafts in 1960. Because limestone is a permeable rock there was a danger of water seeping into the workings. This was prevented by freezing the water in the rock until a concrete lining to the shafts had been built.

Another difficulty which had to be overcome was that of recruiting workers. As Kellingley

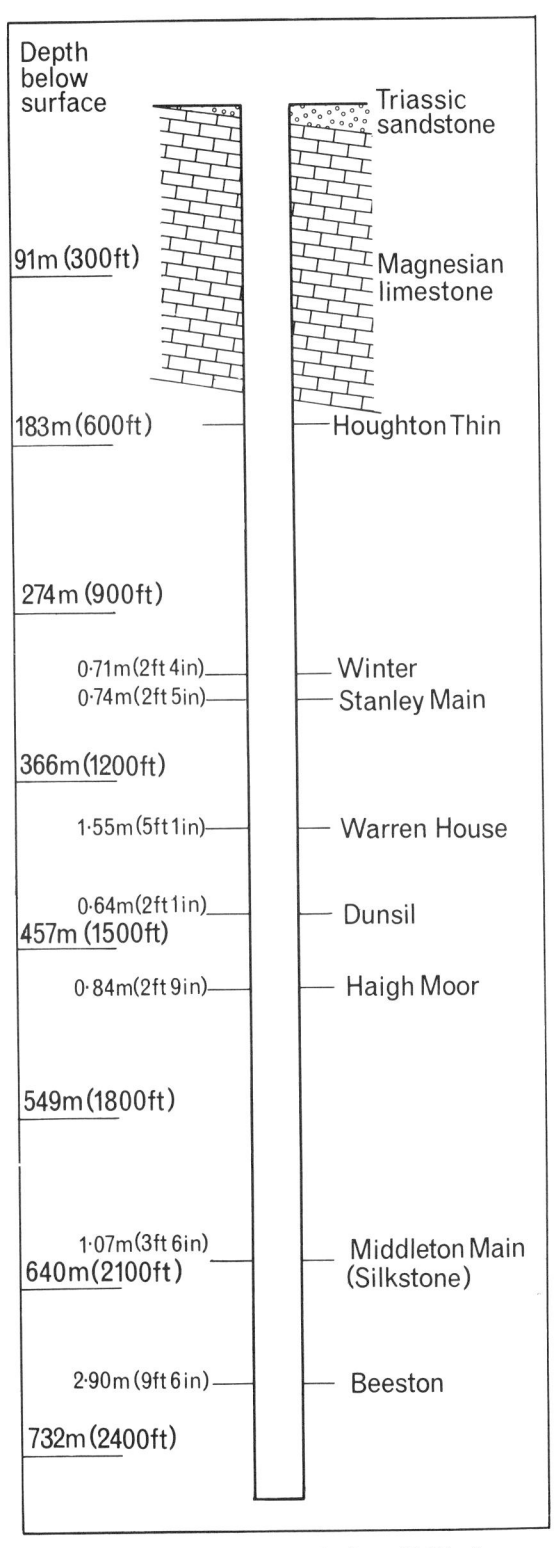

Depth below surface		
		Triassic sandstone
91m (300ft)		
		Magnesian limestone
183m (600ft)		Houghton Thin
274m (900ft)		
0·71m (2ft 4in)		Winter
0·74m (2ft 5in)		Stanley Main
366m (1200ft)		
1·55m (5ft 1in)		Warren House
0·64m (2ft 1in)		Dunsil
457m (1500ft)		
0·84m (2ft 9in)		Haigh Moor
549m (1800ft)		
1·07m (3ft 6in)		Middleton Main (Silkstone)
640m (2100ft)		
2·90m (9ft 6in)		Beeston
732m (2400ft)		

61 *A section through the shaft at Kellingley Colliery*

is several kilometres from the other collieries there were no miners living locally. Men from pits which have closed down in other parts of Britain have been encouraged to move to Kellingley. Lodging fees and travel allowances have been paid to men temporarily separated from their families. Removal expenses have been paid and Knottingley Urban District Council have helped to provide housing.

Eventually the colliery will provide work for 1,600 men who will produce 2 million tonnes of coal a year. About 85 per cent of this coal will probably be sold to power stations for producing electricity. Kellingley is near to several large new power stations. More than half of Yorkshire's coal output is sold to the Central Electricity Generating Board.

Other Yorkshire Collieries

The map (Fig 62) shows that Kellingley lies towards the eastern edge of the Yorkshire Coalfield as do several large collieries around Doncaster. In the centre between Barnsley and Doncaster and in the Castleford–Wakefield district are found most of the other large pits. Further west are the smaller ones and those which have been closed. Notice too that the larger towns of the West Yorkshire lie west of the area where coal is still worked. Fig 63 helps to explain these patterns.

Coal seams are the thin layers of coal found amongst the sandstones, shales and clays which outcrop over much of West Yorkshire. All these rocks are together known as the Coal Measures. Notice how they lie in a basin to the east of the Pennines. Towards the Vales of Trent and York they are covered by younger rocks and form the concealed coalfield. Collieries in this area, like Kellingley and those around Doncaster, are larger and newer than those further west. Where the Coal Measures appear at the surface they form the exposed coalfield. Some of the best conditions for mining are found in the eastern part of the exposed coalfield. Fig 63 shows that this is where the seams are greatest in number and where there is no cover of younger rocks for the shafts to penetrate. Further west, seams are less in number because of the basin-like arrangement of the rocks. In this western part of the coalfield, men have been able for hundreds of years to dig coal

67

with very simple tools from shallow pits. Small mounds of waste, now grassed over, are all that remain of these early workings. The pits still open near the western edge of the coalfield are usually older than those further east. When the National Coal Board took over the industry in 1947, they made many old pits more efficient by installing modern machinery. Others had to be closed because their costs of production were too high or because they were running out of coal.

The difficulties of mining in the west are

62 The Yorkshire Coalfield

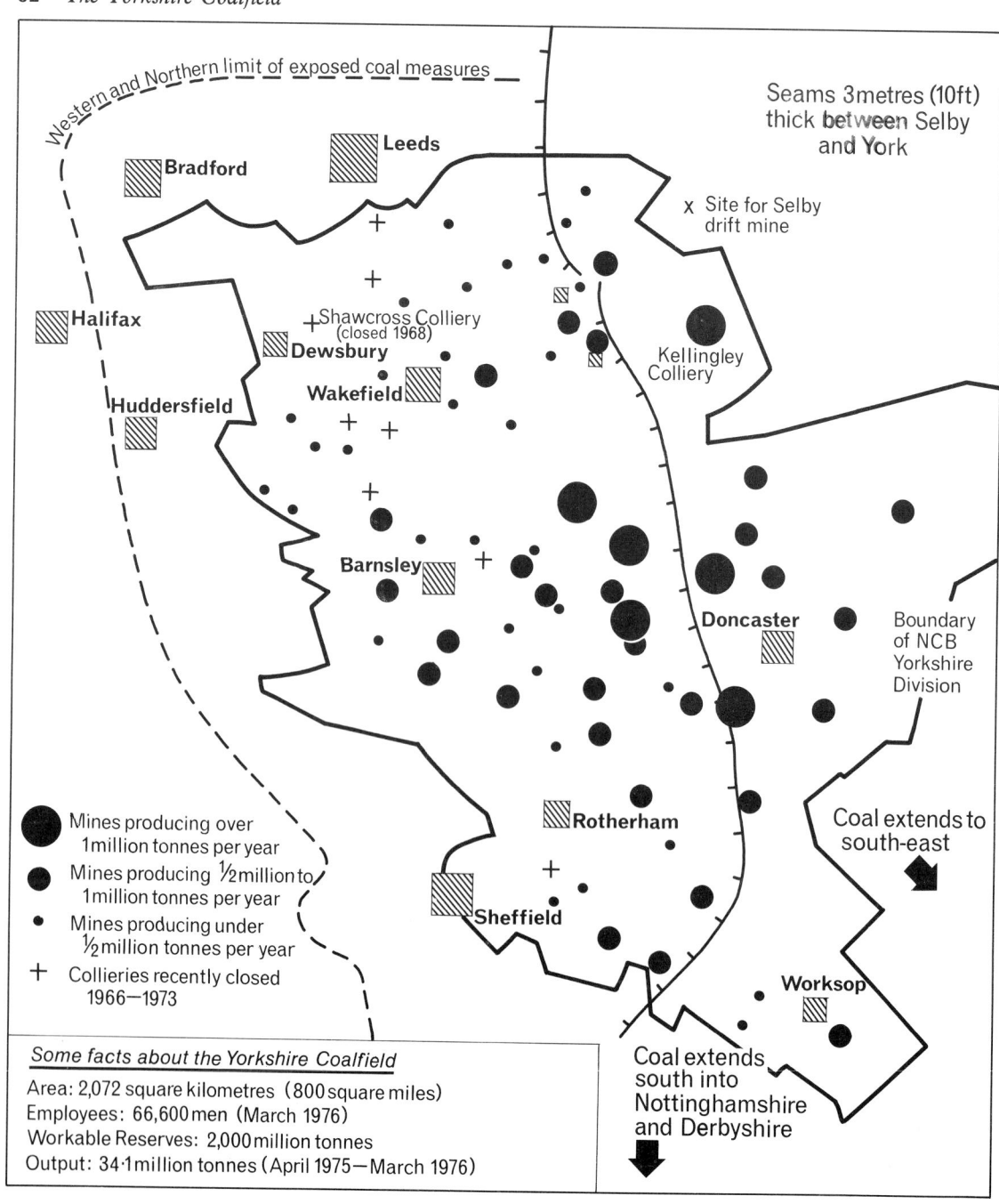

Some facts about the Yorkshire Coalfield
Area: 2,072 square kilometres (800 square miles)
Employees: 66,600 men (March 1976)
Workable Reserves: 2,000 million tonnes
Output: 34·1 million tonnes (April 1975 – March 1976)

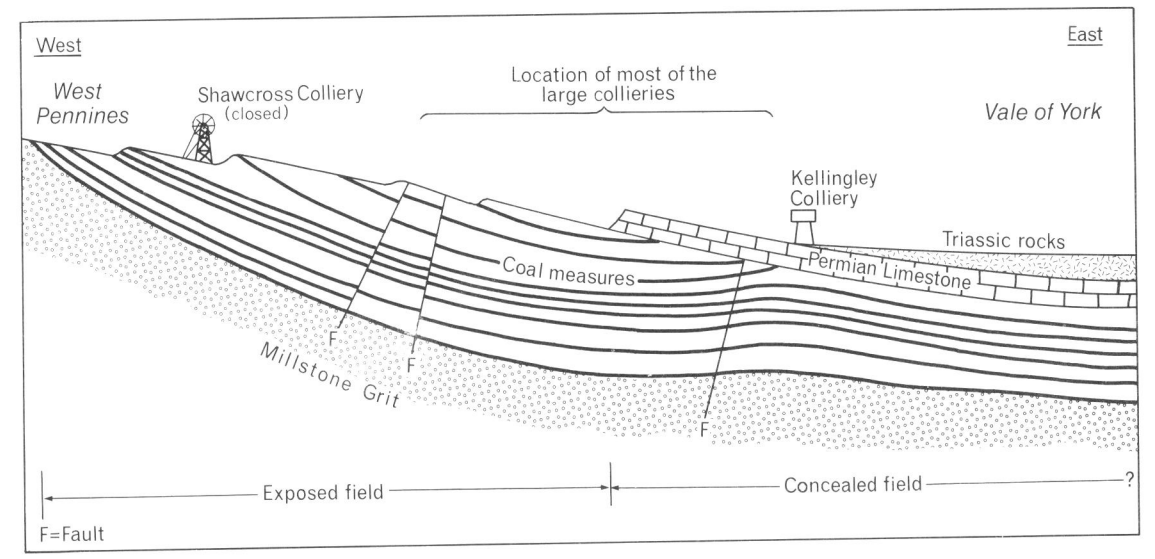

63 *A diagrammatic section through the Yorkshire Coalfield*

64 *Shawcross Colliery 'Take'*

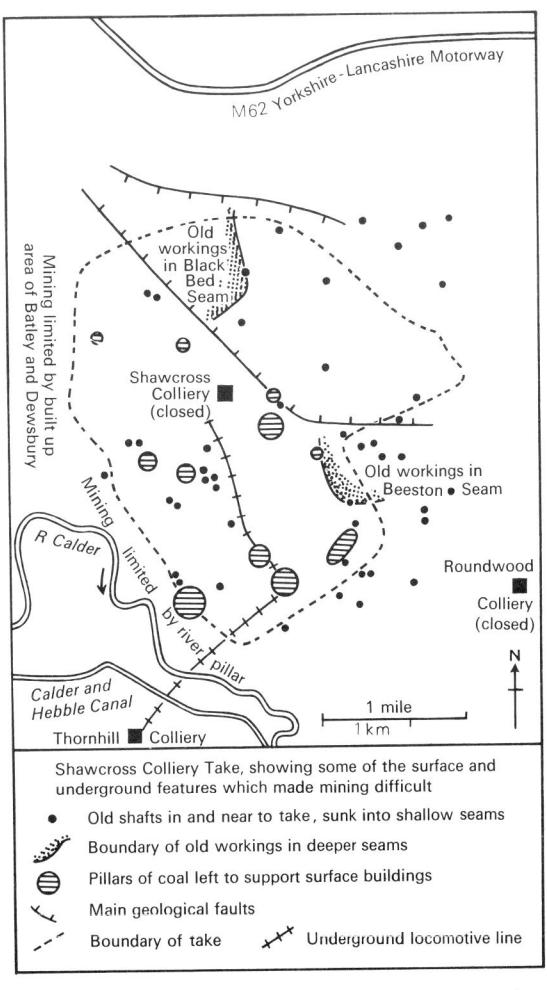

shown by Fig 64. Shawcross Colliery near Dewsbury was sunk in 1872 and in 1967 produced more than 205,500 tonnes of coal. In 1968, the N.C.B. decided to close the pit because the reserves of coal which could be worked economically were almost exhausted. Notice the old shafts from which coal was worked many years ago. These made it difficult and even dangerous to work coal from the shallower seams because of the risk of water flooding in from the old galleries. After the Lofthouse colliery disaster in 1973, the N.C.B. speeded up the work of filling in old shafts. Even in the deeper seams, 'pillars' of coal had to be left under large buildings to prevent them being damaged by subsidence. Mining also had to be avoided under the built up area of Dewsbury. When the colliery closed, the miners were all offered jobs in other parts of the coalfield. Those over sixty years old were offered an early retirement.

Customers for Yorkshire Coal

The Coalfield produces over one quarter of the national output and new developments such as the working of the large reserves in the Selby area will ensure the coalfield's importance long after the year 2000. The coalfield produces a wide range of coals for steam raising, coking, domestic and general industrial use. Fig 65 shows the main consumers of Yorkshire coal. Notice that

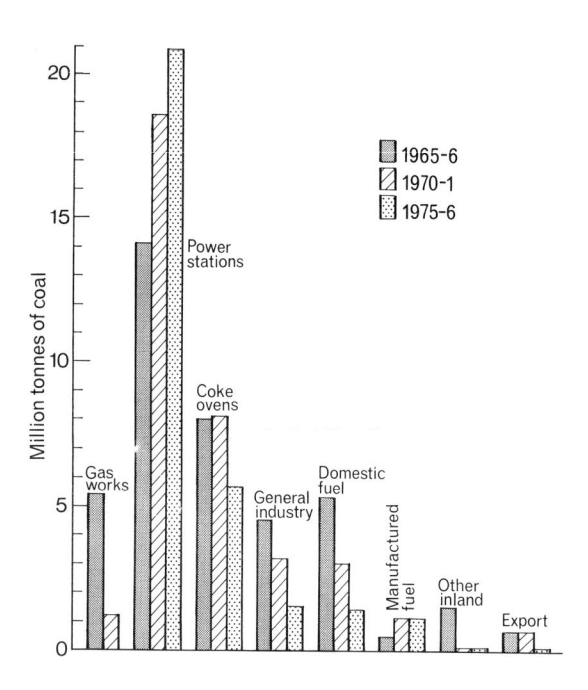

65 Sales of Yorkshire Coal to the main customers

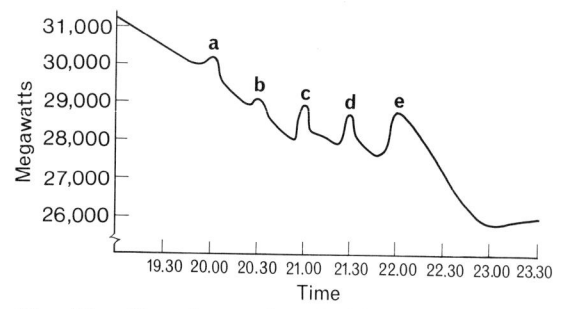

66 The effect of a popular television programme on electricity demand. Peaks **a** and **e** coincide with the start and finish of the film; peaks **b**, **c** and **d** with commercial breaks

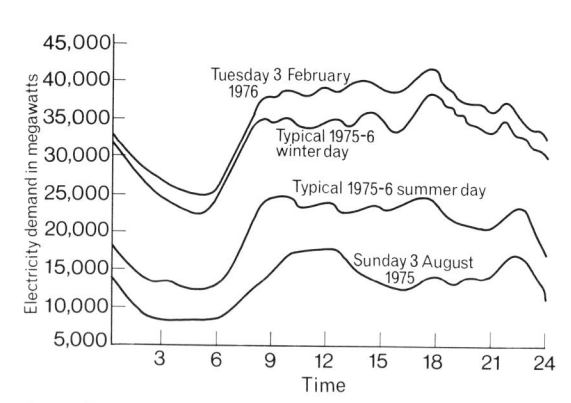

67 Summer and winter electricity demand in 1975–76 including days of maximum and minimum demands

industry and domestic users are buying less coal than they once did. The decline in the demand for housecoal is the result of Smoke Control Zones, central heating and North Sea Gas. Coking coal is sold to the iron and steel industry for coke ovens and to producers such as National Smokeless Fuels.

The biggest customer for Yorkshire coal is the Central Electricity Generating Board. The large Yorkshire power stations convert coal's energy into electricity. Although some electricity is produced in the British Isles by using nuclear energy, water power, and oil, coal is still burnt in most British power stations. Yorkshire, with its ample coal reserves, has become an important producer of electricity and coal is also sent to power stations in Lancashire and Nottinghamshire by rail, road and canal.

The Demand for Electricity

During the evening of 28 October 1975 the James Bond film *Dr No* was shown on British television for the first time. Figure 66 shows the effect of such a popular TV programme on electricity demand. During commercial breaks and at the end of the programme the need for electricity increases as people get up to switch on fires, lights, kettles and other electrical appliances. Figure 67 shows how the demand for electricity changes during typical days. Notice how the demand goes up after about 6.00 a.m. as people start to cook breakfast and machines in factories are switched on at the start of work.

Since electricity cannot be stored in large amounts, it must be produced as it is needed. To do this, the C.E.G.B. must try to estimate demand by studying, among other things, the demand on the same date in the previous year, the weather forecast, television programmes and the hours of daylight. Once the amount of electricity which might be needed at any time has been estimated, instructions are sent to power stations to switch generators on or off. Because the newer stations are the most efficient at converting the energy in coal into electricity they are kept running for most of the time while the older stations, which are more expensive to run, operate only during times of peak demand.

Ferrybridge 'C' Power Station

Ferrybridge 'C' is one of the newer stations and stands with the older Ferrybridge 'B' station between Castleford and Knottingley where the A1 and M62 intersect. The old Ferrybridge 'A' station has now been closed. Figure 68 shows Ferrybridge 'C' in the foreground with Ferrybridge 'B' behind it.

When the 'C' station is working at full power approximately 40 million gallons of water a day are drawn from the River Aire and passed through the condensers to cool the steam which drives the turbo-generators (the huge dynamos which generate the electricity). This large volume of water must then be cooled by the station's eight cooling towers before it can be recirculated through the condensers.

Most of the fuel for the station comes from the Yorkshire coalfield. Each week about 70,000 tons of coal is burnt. Some of this is delivered by rail using the 'merry-go-round' system which is a shuttle service of coal trains running between the power stations and the collieries. Each train is automatically emptied without stopping, to provide a constant supply of coal. Some coal comes to the station by canal in 'trains' of specially made barges. A barge tippler lifts the barge from the water, turns it upside down over a concrete hopper to empty out the coal and then returns the empty barge to the water.

From the unloading points, coal is taken to the boiler house by conveyors. It is then crushed to a fine powder and blown into the boilers where it burns like a gas. Ash falls to the bottom of the boiler while waste gases and dust are drawn into the precipitators which extract the dust before the gases pass up the chimney. The ash is pumped as slurry to Brotherton Ings—a marshy area not far to the north. The dust is pumped in slurry form through a 10 kilometre pipeline to the main disposal area at Gale Common, next to the M62, where the 2000MW Eggborough Power Station is sited.

Steam passes from the boilers to the turbine house to turn the four turbo-generators, each of which can make 500 MW of electricity. Before the electricity passes into the overhead transmission lines, transformers raise its voltage or 'pressure' to 275,000 volts. This allows large

Fig 68 *Ferrybridge 'C' Power Station*

1 Cooling towers   2 Barge Unloader   3 Rail Wagon Unloader   4 Merry-go-round train   5 Coal Conveyor   6 Coal Stock   7 Boiler house   8 Precipitators   9 Turbine hall   10 275 KV Indoor substation   11 Pylons carrying tranmission lines   12 Ferrybridge 'B' power station

amounts of power to be transmitted without having very thick cables. It is rather like pushing a lot of water through a narrow pipe by pumping it at very high pressure. In the centre of the photograph (Fig 68) is the indoor substation where switches, worked from a control room, regulate the flow of electricity into the cables. The grid system, as the nationwide network of transmission lines is called, carries power at high voltage from Ferrybridge 'C' and other power stations to users in all parts of the country. Fig 69 shows how this is done. The Area Electricity Board receives the power at 132,000 volts for distribution to consumers. However, the construction of the 400,000 volt supergrid has now made it possible for power to be moved long distances from where it can be made cheaply, like the Yorkshire Coalfield, to factories and towns in other areas without having too many cables crisscrossing the countryside. For one pylon 50 metres high, carrying a 400,000 volt line, transmits as much power as four 41.5 metre pylons carrying 275,000 volt lines or eighteen 27 metre pylons carrying 132,000 volt lines.

Other Power Stations in North Yorkshire and Humberside

The Ferrybridge 'B' station was opened in 1957 and can produce 300 MW of electricity while the 'C' station, opened in 1966, can produce 2000 MW. The 'C' station is one of three very large stations in this area which were built to take advantage of the large resources of the eastern part of the Yorkshire coalfield which will be able to supply coal for many years, especially with the discovery of the thick coal seams between York and Selby. Also the lower courses of the river provide sufficient cooling water and the flat open sites along their banks are free from mining subsidence and therefore ideal for large buildings, railway tracks and the other equipment of a modern power station.

The other two large power stations are at Eggborough 8 km (5 miles) east of Ferrybridge and at Drax on the river Ouse between Selby and Goole. Most of the smaller stations lie in the south-west of Yorkshire near the big towns. Many of these were working before the grid system was built and it was then essential for them to be near the towns where the electricity was used. After nationalisation of the electricity industry in 1948 the grid system was greatly expanded which made it possible for the big new stations to be built away from the towns and nearer to the supplies of coal. With the new stations completed the Yorkshire and Humberside region is able to produce 9500 MW of electricity which is more than is used in the region so much of it is 'exported' through the grid system to other parts of Britain.

69 *How electricity reaches the home*

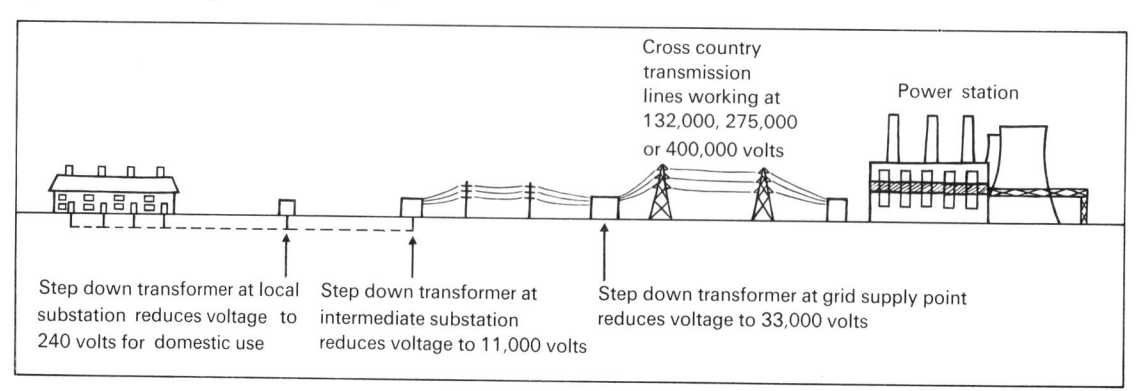

Work to do
1. Why has coal output in Britain declined in recent years? What are the arguments for increasing coal output in the future?
2. Study Figs 62 and 63 then explain:
   (a) why the recently closed collieries are in the west of the Yorkshire coalfield
   (b) why the biggest and most productive collieries are in the east.

3. The map below shows the area where a thick seam of coal has been confirmed in boreholes to the north and west of Selby. The coalfield will be exploited from a drift mine at the disused Gascoigne Wood Marshalling Yard, where 10 million tonnes of coal will be brought to the surface annually. Construction work began in autumn 1976. Discuss reasons for choosing this site for the mine entrance, loading bunkers for liner trains, coal stocking areas and a coal preparation plant. What advantages and problems will the mine bring to this rural area?

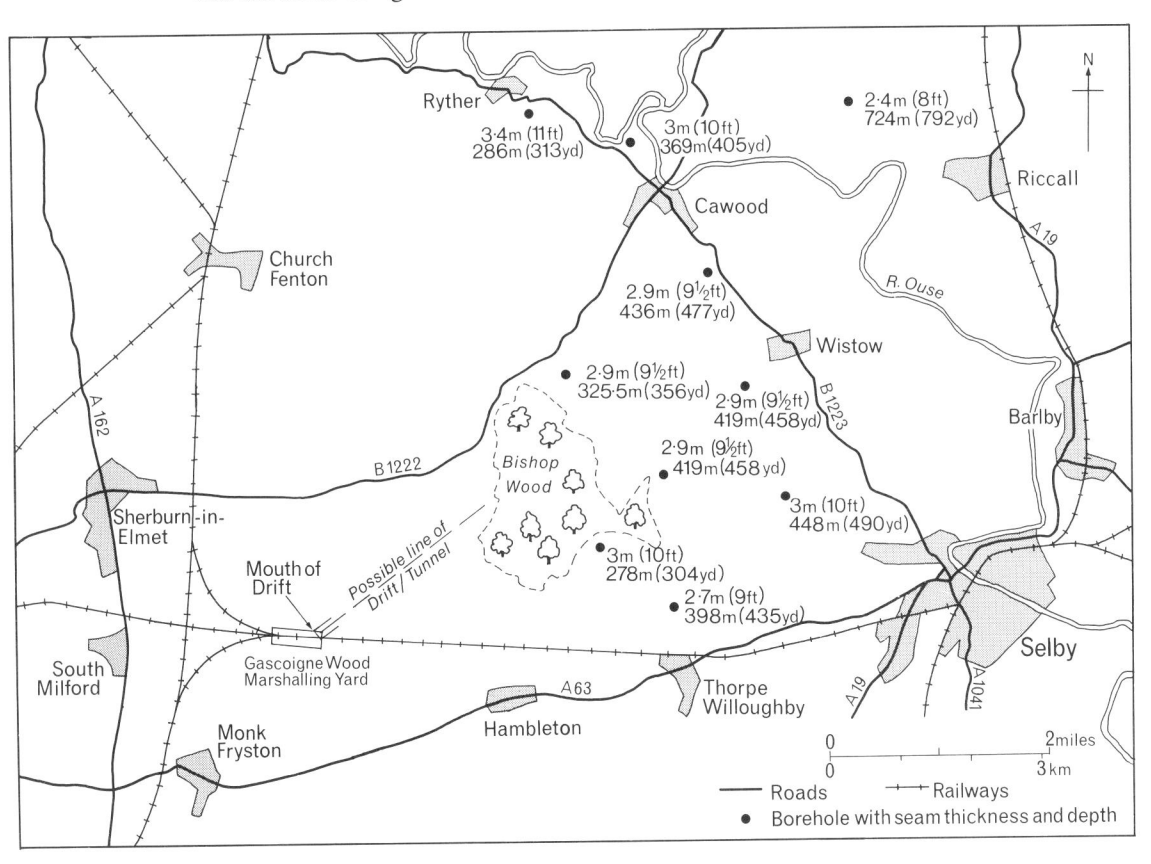

4. Keep a log of the consumption of electricity in your home by noting when different appliances are switched on and off. Does your use of electricity conform to any of the patterns of demand shown in Figs. 66 and 67?
5. Make a list of the advantages of the Ferrybridge district for electricity production. If there is a power station near your home, compare its site with that of Ferrybridge.
6. What would have been the advantages and disadvantages of building a nuclear powered station in this area instead of the proposed second stage to the coal powered station at Drax?

9 | SHEFFIELD AND THE DON VALLEY

70 The Park Hill and Hyde Park redevelopment areas

The Park Hill and Hyde Park Redevelopment Areas

Fig 70 is a photograph of the Park Hill and Hyde Park redevelopment areas. The taller building in the distance is the Hyde Park development and the larger lower one is Park Hill.

The redevelopment of Sheffield's housing began seriously in 1952. The Park Hill—Hyde Park housing complex, which is right in the heart of the city, replaced 800 slum houses with 2,207 new dwellings. This was one of Britain's first inner cities to be redeveloped after the war using new concepts of planning and the project won high praise both nationally and internationally. Other neighbourhood re-developments have taken place since on a similar pattern at Netherthorpe, Woodside, Burngreave, Lansdowne and Kelvin (see Fig 72). Kelvin, for example, has 945 dwellings, a shopping precinct, welfare centre as well as providing special facilities for the disabled.

At Park Hill bridges link the blocks at every third floor where there is also a pedestrian street deck. Every dwelling opens on to one of these so that milk trolleys can be driven along them and people can visit neighbours or go shopping with their prams. Goods and passenger lifts serve all floors. The dwellings are not all the same. Some are flats for only one person while others are maisonettes for families of six, but all have a private balcony, a modern bathroom and kitchen. Notice the tall chimney of the boiler house which provides hot water and central heating for all the homes.

The plan of Park Hill (Fig 71) shows that between the blocks are large open spaces which are set out as gardens and play areas. Residents also have easy access to the nearby park. Notice the shopping centre, schools and other amenities, all near to the dwellings. There are coffee bars and public houses, while clubs of all kinds can hold meetings and run dances in a modern hall.

The Growth of Sheffield

Sheffield, like many of Yorkshire's industrial cities, grew into a large town during the Industrial Revolution between 1750 and 1850. At this time people had to live near to their work-place because there was no public transport. This led to overcrowding in the central areas. Houses spread quickly up the hillsides from the factories on the valley floors. To save space and money they were built back to back.

71 *The layout of the Park Hill development*

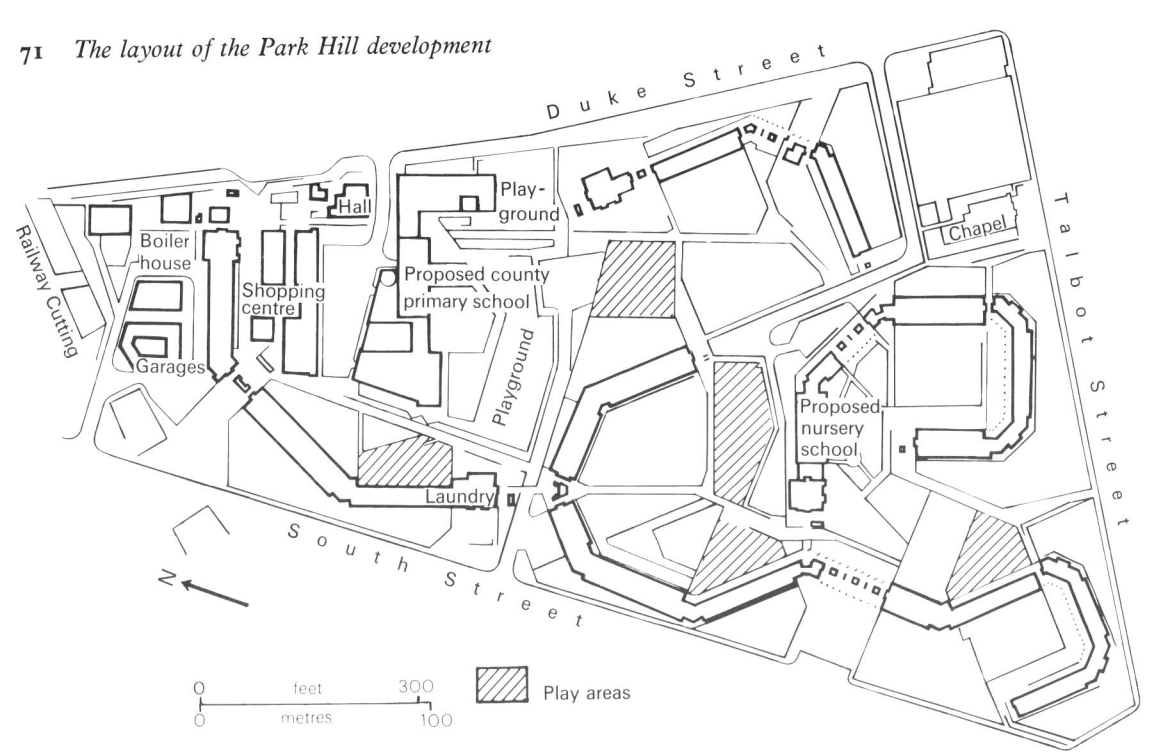

More recently, buses and motor cars have made it possible for people to live well away from their work. Between the wars (1918–39) Sheffield Corporation built housing estates, like those at Shiregreen, Parson's Cross and Arbourthorne on the outskirts of the city. Each house had a bathroom, lavatory and gardens. At the same time, private-house building was taking place especially in the hills and wooded valleys to the west. In recent years, most slum houses have been demolished and their occupants rehoused in new estates on the southern outskirts or in multi-storey blocks near the city centre.

The Centre of Sheffield

The Park Hill—Hyde Park area is one of five where slums have been replaced by large blocks of modern dwellings. Fig 72 shows they stand on the three broad spurs which meet where the Sheaf flows into the Don. The inhabitants are within a mile of the city centre and close to, but windward of, the factories alongside the River Don.

The map shows that the main buildings of the city are on a broad spur between the Don and Sheaf. In the twelfth century the Norman,

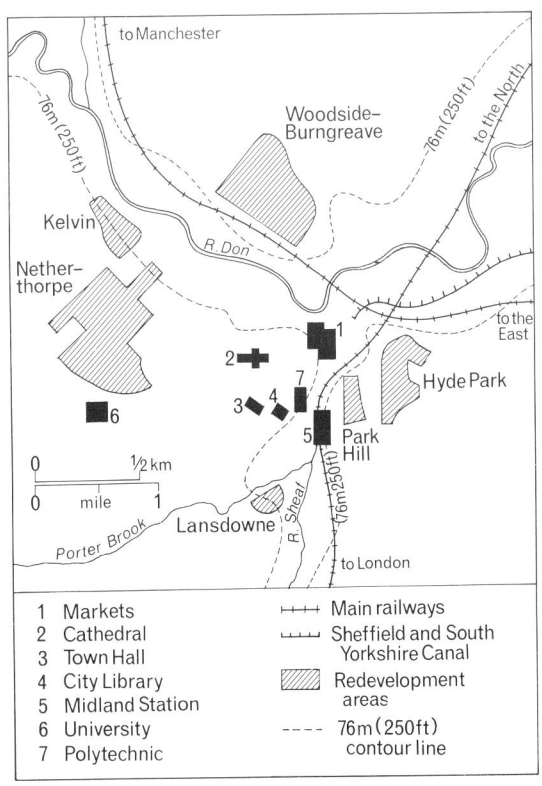

1 Markets
2 Cathedral
3 Town Hall
4 City Library
5 Midland Station
6 University
7 Polytechnic

Main railways
Sheffield and South Yorkshire Canal
Redevelopment areas
76m (250ft) contour line

72 *The centre of Sheffield with the redevelopment areas*

William de Lovetot, built a castle here overlooking Lady's Bridge. The Norfolk Market stands on the Castle Hill today. A parish church, now the Cathedral, was built on the hill behind and a market place grew up beside the castle.

The present Castle Market Hall is on the site of a large department store, which, like many other buildings in the city, was destroyed by bombs during the Second World War. The photograph in Fig 73 shows the Market Hall, a seven-storey office block, and stairways leading to shops on balconies above street level. There is a bridge which allows shoppers to cross the busy street in safety. Ideas of this kind are to be found in many city centres which are being rebuilt.

Fig 74 is a map of Sheffield showing the central business district and the main housing and industrial areas. The central business district, with shops, offices, banks, hotels and cinemas, has grown up around the old castle and cathedral site. Housing occupies the surrounding hills but avoids the steep valley sides, e.g. in the Rivelin Valley. Industry is found mainly on the Don Valley floor where steel making and heavy en-

73 *The Castle Market and other new developments at the junction of Exchange Street and the Haymarket*

74 *The built-up areas of Sheffield*

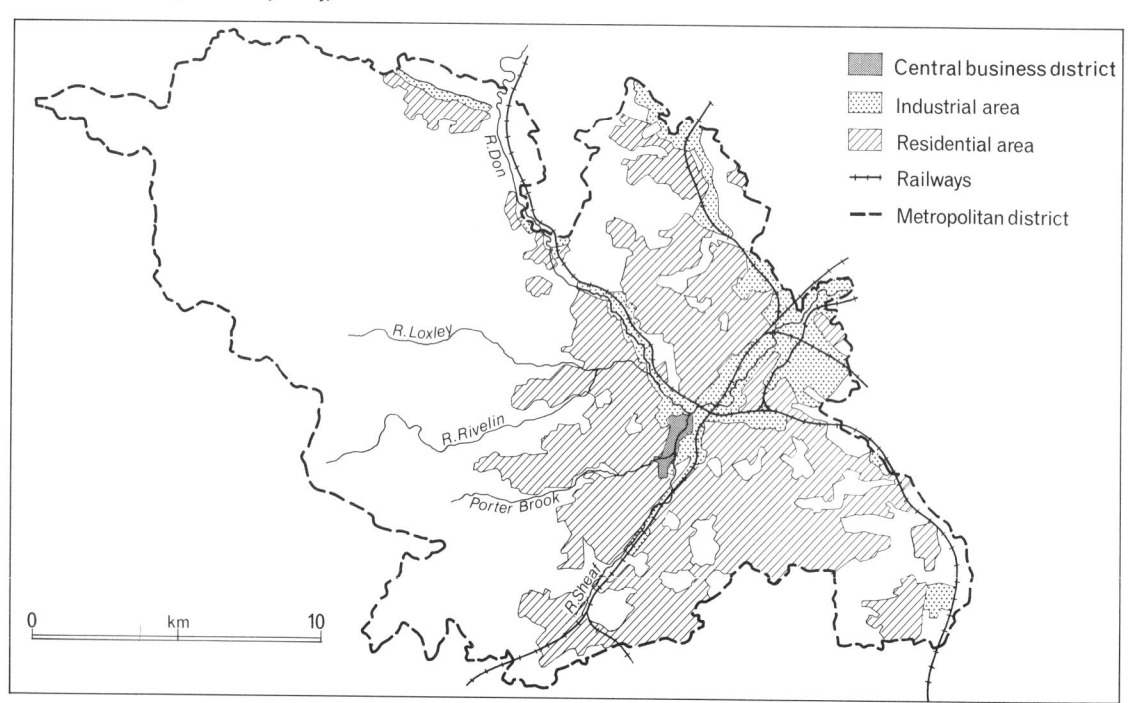

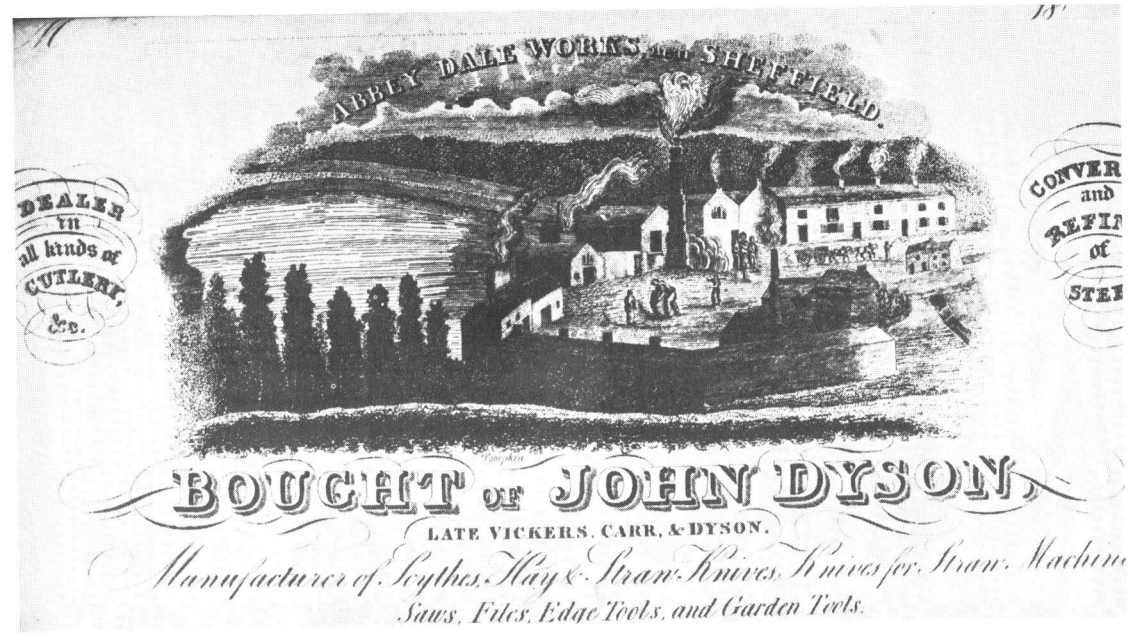

75 An old print of the Abbeydale Scythe Works

76 Craftsmen at work at old works of Joseph Rogers and Sons Ltd.

gineering are carried on. The small industrial areas to the west and south-west of the city centre contain many of the cutlery works for which Sheffield is world famous.

The Cutlery Industry
Cutlery includes not only tableware but a whole range of cutting tools such as scissors, razors and surgical instruments. Records show that cutlery has been made in Sheffield since at least the fourteenth century.

The earliest cutlers had small workshops, containing anvils and a small furnace, attached to their cottages. As trade grew, the Upper Don and its tributaries were used to drive water wheels. These powered grindstones, tilt hammers and furnace bellows. The wooded valley slopes provided charcoal for smelting and iron ore was obtained in small quantities from the Coal Measure rocks. High quality iron and steel was imported from as far away as Sweden, Spain and Russia. One of the old works which used water power has been restored as an industrial museum at Abbeydale in the Sheaf Valley.

The Abbeydale Works is an eighteenth century scythe works, five and a half kilometres (three

77 *The Don Valley at Tinsley between Sheffield and Rotherham looking north-west*

and a half miles) south-west of the city centre. The monks of Beauchief Abbey worked mills along this part of the River Sheaf in the thirteenth century but the oldest buildings remaining at Abbeydale date from 1785. The curator of the Museum found the old print of the works shown in Fig 75 in the Sheffield Directory of 1833. On the left is the mill pond, fed by the Sheaf, which provided water to turn the wheels. There were many such water wheels on the Don tributaries at one time and the old mill ponds still remain in the western valleys.

The buildings at Abbeydale are grouped round a courtyard. They include workers' cottages, a row of forges where craftsmen finished scythe blades and hand forged other articles from steel bars, and a grinding shop, powered by a $5\frac{1}{2}$-metre (18-foot) diameter waterwheel. The buildings next to the millpond are the crucible steel melting shop, the hardening shop, the tilt shop and the boring shop.

In the melting shop, high quality steel was made by a process invented by Benjamin Huntsman in 1742. He was a Lincolnshire clockmaker who settled in Sheffield and his invention made the area an important steel centre. The tilt shop

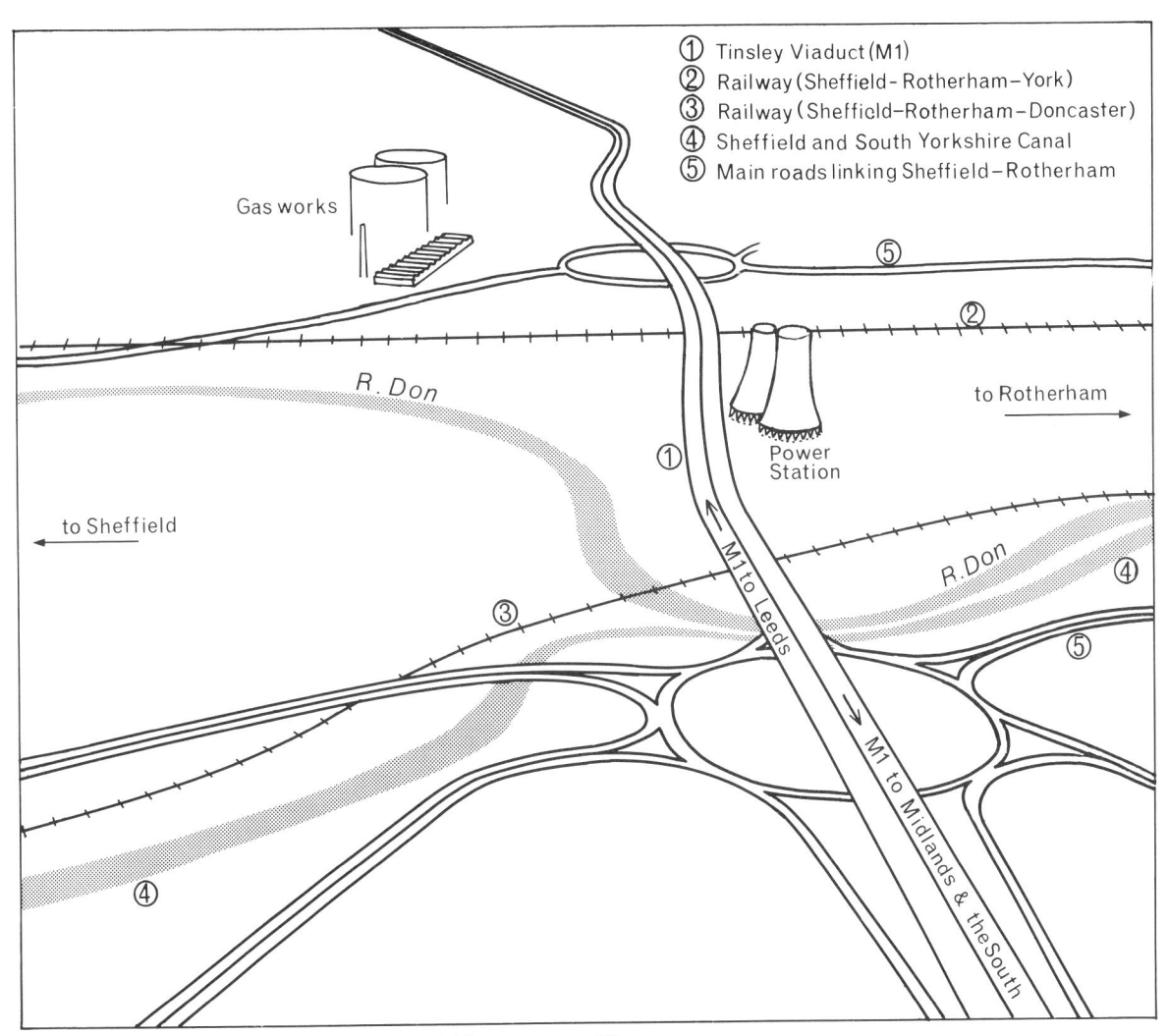

78 *A sketch to show the main routes which appear on Fig 77*

contained the tilt hammers. Here, cogs on a revolving mainshaft raised, and then allowed to fall, the large hammers used to shape scythe and other blades.

The Abbeydale works closed in 1933, but many water powered works shut much earlier as steam engines were used more and more. Today cutlery is made in small factories within one and a half kilometres (one mile) and to the west of the city centre. Many started as backyard workshops behind houses built in the late eighteenth century. The firm of Joseph Rodgers began in this way. As trade grew, it moved, in 1882, to the larger works on the River Sheaf in the town centre which have now been demolished.

Fig 76 shows craftsmen at work in the old Rodgers factory assembling stockmen's knives from parts made in the other departments. Notice the many hand tools, the vice and a small anvil. The making of a quality penknife needs almost 200 separate operations. Machines now do many of them but skilled men and women are still needed to assemble and polish the cutlery by hand. The factory has now moved further up the Sheaf valley and the old site has been redeveloped by the Post Office.

Sheffield factories make other small metal goods as well as cutlery. The table below shows only a few of those listed in the Sheffield and District Classified Telephone Directory.

	Number of Companies
Tool makers	110
Wire makers	16
Silversmiths	32
Machine tool makers	24
Electroplate manufacturers	2
Bolt and nut manufacturers	26

Steel Making and Heavy Engineering

Fig 77 is an air photograph of the Don Valley near to Sheffield's boundary with Rotherham, looking north-west. Fig 78 helps to explain it. Running diagonally across the photograph is the Tinsley Viaduct. It has two decks to carry the Yorkshire section of the M1 and a local road across the congested valley floor.

Older means of communication can be seen running along the valley floor. Notice the canal which opened in 1819 to link Sheffield via the River Don to the Humber. The first railway link between Sheffield and Rotherham opened in 1838 and can be seen on the far side of the valley. On the slopes are terraces of older houses, newer semi-detached ones and modern blocks of flats. Notice too the gas works, Blackburn Meadows Power Station, and on the right of the picture the sewage works. In the distance are the steep wooded slopes of a tributary valley.

Many of the factories which crowded the valley between Sheffield and Rotherham can be seen in the photograph. In the nineteenth century, steel and engineering works were built here on flat land near to the canal and the railway. The steelmakers came from smaller works in the narrow western tributary valleys as well as from other parts of the country. They were anxious to expand their businesses to meet the growing demand for iron and steel for railways, ships, armaments and all kinds of engineering products.

The River Don Works, Brightside

The River Don Works of the British Steel Corporation is one of the biggest in the area, employing approximately 3,000 workers. It is part of the B.S.C.'s Forges, Foundries, and Engineering Profit Centre which has other works throughout the country and in Sheffield. Fig 79 shows that the works stands on flat land beside the River Don. On its northern side runs the Sheffield–Rotherham railway. Inside the works, railways are used to carry large steel ingots, forgings and castings into the machine shops where they are handled by large overhead cranes.

Notice on Fig 79 the coal-fired power stations which make some of the electricity for the electric-arc furnaces, heavy machine tools and hydraulic presses. In 1902 the old North Gun-shop had electric motors installed to drive its machine tools. In the nineteenth century steam engines and water wheels on the River Don had provided the power. The river water was also used for cooling as it is today.

Sheffield and the Don Valley cannot compete in the production of cheap steel with coastal areas such as Teesside and Scunthorpe which can import foreign ore cheaply. The Parkgate Works, Rotherham, the last in the area to have blast furnaces, ceased smelting iron ore in 1974. The steel furnaces at the River Don Works, and at others in the area, are 'charged' with steel scrap and a small percentage of cold pig iron. The melted 'charge' is analysed and then has other materials added to make high grade alloy steels to a required specification. These special steels are used to make engineering products which must stand up to very high pressures and speeds, great heat and constant wear. Examples are power station turbines, pressure vessels for the chemical industry, and jet engines. The steel is cast into ingots of up to 210 tonnes and taken to the forging shops. Here it is reheated before being 'squeezed' by huge presses into a rough shape ready for machining. This process improves the quality of the steel.

Before machining the steel is heat treated. In the machine shops the forgings are then turned or ground on lathes and grinding machines to exact sizes. A vast range of products is made, from diesel engine crankshafts to huge components like the turbine shaft shown in Fig 80. It is 1·2 metres (4 feet) in diameter and is made of nickel–chrome–molybdenum steel. It was ordered by the Hydro-Electric Power Commis-

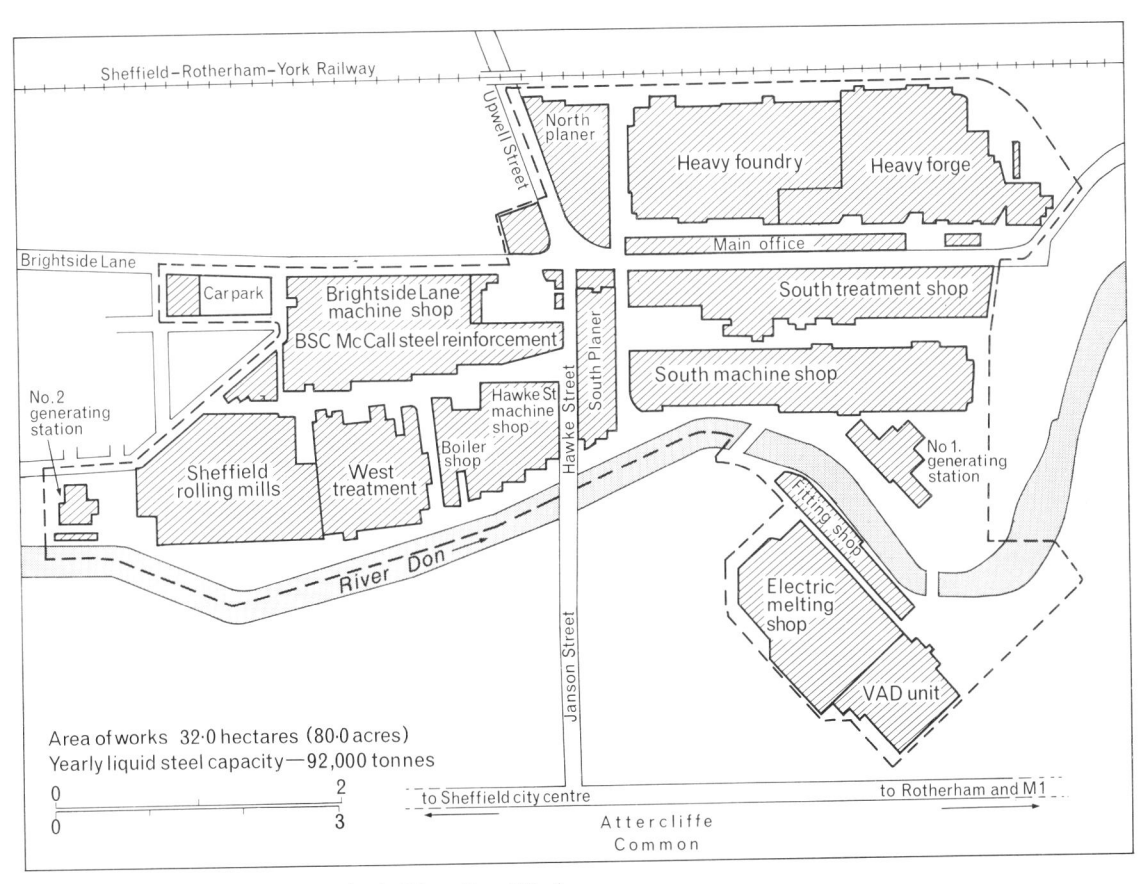

79 *The British Steel Corporation's River Don Works.*

sion of Ontario, Canada. Notice the huge lathe being controlled by one man.

Before becoming part of the publicly owned B.S.C., the River Don Works was part of the English Steel Corporation which was formed in 1929 when the shipbuilding and armaments interests of the Armstrong Whitworth, Vickers, and Cammell Laird companies merged. These had been producing steel, armour and guns at Sheffield and Manchester for their shipyards at Walker-on-Tyne, Barrow and Birkenhead as well as many other steel goods.

In 1964 the English Steel Corporation built a modern steel alloy plant at Tinsley Park. This now produces up to 350,000 tonnes of special steel bullets and bars per annum.

The most recent B.S.C. development in Sheffield is the modernised stainless steel plant at Tinsley Park and Shepcote Lane. This will be completed in 1978 and will then produce up to 55,000 tonnes of stainless steel plate and 165,000 tonnes of cold rolled sheet and coil stainless steel per year.

Work to do
1. From a large scale plan of part of your town, or a Yorkshire town, make sketches of the layout of (i) back-to-back houses, (ii) modern council houses, (iii) multi-storey flats.
2. What are the advantages and disadvantages of multi-storey housing developments and shopping precincts like those at Park Hill? If there are similar redevelopment schemes in your town carry out a survey on what people think about them and write a report on your findings.

80 *A power station shaft being machined on a lathe in the River Don Works of the British Steel Corporation.*

3. Study Figs 72 and 74 and then describe how relief features have affected the growth of Sheffield.
4. Using a large scale street plan, make a map of part of your own town showing it divided into housing, industrial and service areas. This could be done from a classified telephone directory and by visiting the chosen area.
5. From a copy of the official handbook, 'City of Sheffield' or a classified telephone directory, make a list of the products of Sheffield's industries.
6. List the reasons for the growth of metal-working industries in the valleys west of Sheffield before 1850.
7. Draw a sketch map of the section of the Don Valley shown in Fig 77. Label the river, canal, railways, and main roads. Shade the main factories and any housing areas.
8. The figures below show the approximate numbers of people in certain occupations in South Yorkshire in 1971. The figures are for the more important centres only.

	Barnsley	Mexborough & Goldthorpe	Rotherham	Sheffield	Doncaster
Mining and quarrying	5,900	11,300	4,000	2,800	17,700
Metal manufacture	1,500	700	15,600	39,100	600
Mechanical engineering	1,500	100	3,200	12,100	1,500
Electrical engineering	1,100	—	700	2,800	1,900
Small metal goods, including tools, cutlery, wire, containers and jewellery	1,100	200	700	44,500	4,700

(a) On a sketch map of the Don and its tributary the Dearne, mark the five centres.
(b) Draw bar graphs to show the distribution of the five occupations in South Yorkshire.
(c) Describe the differences between employment in the five centres which are shown by the graph. (d) What forms of employment are available in your home district?

9. Why does the Sheffield area (a) produce much high quality steel but little pig iron; (b) use large quantities of scrap metal in its furnaces?
10. The firm of Joseph Rodgers and Sons Ltd moved from an old factory near the city centre to a site further up the Sheaf Valley. In many towns, light industries have moved to the outskirts. Make a list of advantages they may gain from such a move.
11. On a map of your own town or district, mark the location of any factories built recently. In what kind of locations are they found?

10 | THE WEST YORKSHIRE CONURBATION

The Calder Valley near Halifax

The photograph (Fig 81) was taken from the air looking north-west across the West Yorkshire town of Halifax. Notice the railway station in the foreground of the picture; the power station; the large number of mills with their tall chimneys; the row of terrace houses; the new housing estates on the outskirts of the town. Open countryside risies up to the moorland plateau of the Pennines to the north-west of the town. Most of the buildings near the centre are made of stone which was quarried from the nearby hillsides and many of the older ones are roofed with flagstones. Over the years these materials have been blackened by smoke from the chimneys of factories and houses. However, many of these buildings are now being demolished and replaced with modern blocks of flats, offices and shops. Fig 82 shows a section of the same area taken after the completion of the new inner relief road. Notice that many old buildings have been demolished to make way for the road and how many new build-

81 *Halifax*

ngs there are. Similar changes are taking place in the other industrial towns of Yorkshire.

The Ordnance Survey map (Map D, p. 86) and the relief diagram (Fig 83) cover a small part of the Pennines where Halifax is situated. Here the land forms a plateau which rises to over 305 metres (1,000 feet) in the west and slopes gently down to about 152 metres (500 feet) in the east. The main river, the Calder, flows eastwards in a narrow steep-sided valley. It was deepened during the Ice Age by water from melting glaciers. The valleys of tributaries like Hebble Brook and Red Beck have steeper west-facing sides. These often rise to wooded scarp slopes or 'edges' as at Hove Edge (130242). This is because the rocks here are dipping towards the east.

The main valleys provide the easiest routes through the Pennines and so are used by the railways, canals and many of the major roads. Notice how the 'Calder and Hebble Navigation' canal, a main road and a railway run along the floor of the valley between Brighouse (140220) and Elland (100210). The larger tributary valleys are used in a similar way, though some of the smaller ones, e.g. Red Beck, are followed only by minor roads.

A high density of population is indicated by the number and size of the towns and villages. These are mainly in the valleys though some e.g., Bank Top (105245), have grown up on the plateau. Notice how Halifax, the largest town on the map, stands in the valley of Hebble Brook and not on the Calder. An atlas map will show that many of the other important towns of West Yorkshire lie in tributary valleys of the main rivers. The suburbs of Halifax climb to 300 metres (1,000 feet) up the gentle western side of the valley to the edge of the Pennine moors. Many of the other towns in this part of Yorkshire have grown up the moorland slopes away from the confined sites on the valley floor. Settlements have also expanded to give a continuous line of buildings or 'ribbon development'. A good example of this can be seen along the A641 road from Brighouse north to New Road Side (150270). Often only the boundaries marked on maps show where one town ends and another begins.

The large number of first-class roads, railways and canals and the high density of buildings suggest that the Calder Valley is an industrial

82 Halifax showing section of new inner relief road.

area. Most of the large buildings shown on the map by the side of canals, rivers and streams are factories, particularly where they stand next to small reservoirs. Examples of these can be seen along the stream which flows into the Calder at grid reference 100213. However, the photograph (Fig. 81) shows better than the map how numerous the mills and factories are in this area.

More than 2 million people live in the towns of West Yorkshire which line the valleys of the Aire, Calder, Colne and their tributaries. The Halifax area, as shown in Fig 81 and Map D, is typical of this part of the county.

Making Wool Cloth in West Yorkshire

Four fifths of all the wool textiles made in Britain come from mills in West Yorkshire. Many processes are needed to make the cloths for which the area is world famous. First the raw wool is sorted by skilled workers who look carefully at the fibres before putting those of the same quality into large baskets. At this stage about half the weight of the wool is grease and dirt which must be removed by scouring in tanks of soapy water.

The clean but tangled wool is then passed through carding machines. These consist of large cylinders covered with short projecting wires.

Map D *Part of the OS 1 : 50,000 map sheet 104*

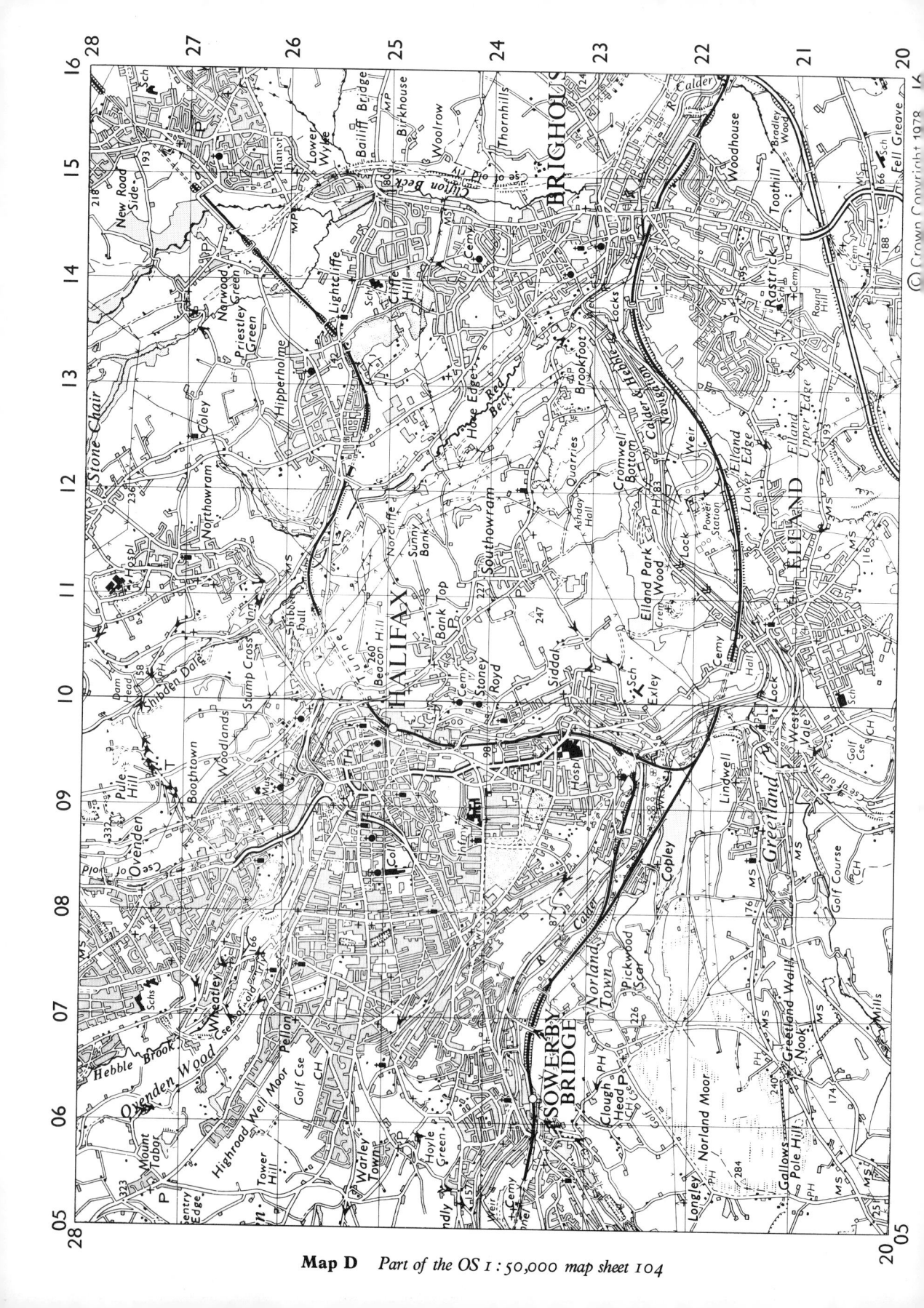

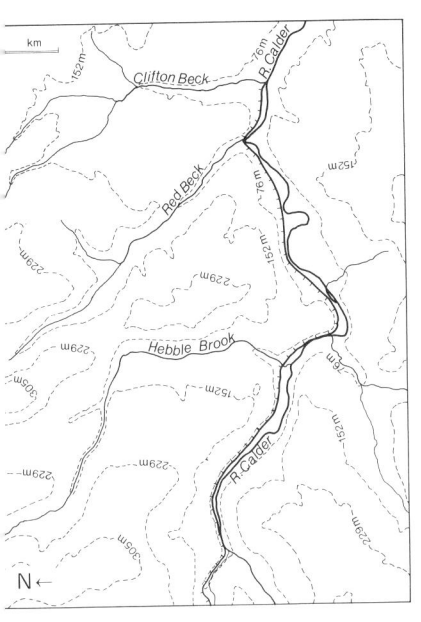

Relief map of the area shown in Map D

As the cylinders rotate at different speeds the wires comb out the wool fibres, which are drawn off in long even bands called slivers. The long fibres or 'tops' are separated by a combing machine from the short fibres or 'noils'; tops are used in making worsteds, which are generally finer than woollens which use noils.

The fibres are then ready to be drawn out and twisted into yarn by spinning machines. These are supervised by workers who repair any broken threads. When the bobbins are full the yarn is ready to be made up into cloth. This is done by intertwining two sets of yarn on a loom which is rather like a huge darning machine. The 'warp' yarn is set up first on the loom and the 'weft' yarn is wound onto a shuttle. This does the job of a darning needle by passing between the threads of the warp. On modern looms several colours can be used to produce a variety of cloth designs.

In the next stage, the rolls of cloth pass through what is called 'burling and mending'. Burling is the removal of any small flaws such as knots, while mending is the sewing in of any damaged parts with matching threads. The cloth is then washed, dried, cropped of any long hairs, ironed, folded, pressed and packed in canvas-covered bales before being despatched from the mills.

Clothing manufacturers all over Britain are supplied by the West Riding mills, though the factories in Leeds are the biggest buyers especially for worsted suitings. The cloth for export is sent to Goole, Hull, London and Liverpool for shipment to all parts of the world.

Only a few of the mills complete all of the cloth-making operations. Many specialise in only one or two stages, the wool passing round from mill to mill until the cloth is finished. The maps (Fig 84) have been drawn from addresses of mills given in classified telephone directories. They show that the wool towns specialise in different branches of the industry. Notice that the mills where worsteds are made are few in the south-east around Wakefield and Dewsbury, but are concentrated in Bradford, Huddersfield, Halifax and the towns of the Aire Valley. The making of woollens is more widely distributed, but is less widespread than worsteds in Bradford, Keighley and Bingley. Most of the mungo and shoddy mills are found in Dewsbury, Batley and Ossett. Mungo is made from old cloth and shoddy from old knitted goods. After being torn up into their original fibres, the different grades of mungo and shoddy are blended with other fibres before being made up into cloth in the usual way.

Dyeing is concentrated in Bradford, the Aire Valley and the valleys of the Colne and the Calder. The floors of many big hotels, famous buildings, ocean liners and millions of homes in Britain and overseas are covered with carpets made in Halifax, Huddersfield and Brighouse.

World wool prices are studied carefully because Bradford merchants have agents in all the main wool-growing countries. The merchants buy wool and ship it to Britain. Nowadays, less than ten per cent of the wool used is British, the rest being imported. Table 5 shows that rather less than a half comes from New Zealand and Australia. South Africa is the third most important supplier and the countries of South America with temperate grasslands are an important source. The finest quality wool comes from Merino sheep which are reared in large numbers in Australia. Wool imports have fallen drastically in recent years because of the increasing use of man-made fibres and of the switch by producing countries to more profitable meat production.

Table 5. *Wool Imports into Britain*

	Million kilos 1976
New Zealand	40·9
Australia	34·0
South Africa	17·0
Argentina	12·0
Brazil	5·6
Uruguay	9·4
Irish Republic	8·7
India and Pakistan	4·6
Others	29·8
	162·0

Fibres from other animals are also imported for making special fabrics. South African mohair from the Angora goat is the most important. Others are cashmere, camel's hair, alpaca, and llama. Man-made or synthetic fibres, e.g. nylon and terylene, are also used in many of the mills. These are often blended with wool to make special types of cloth.

Many changes are taking place in the wool textile industry. Some of the smaller firms have been taken over by larger companies. By this means the mills can be run more efficiently; they can obtain new machines which make cloth more quickly and require fewer workers.

The fine cloths made in Yorkshire depend not only on the skill of its workers but on research as well. The wool industry has its own research association (known as Wira), which was established in 1918. It is based in Leeds and recognised as one of the leading textile research associations in the world. Other research work is carried out in the large mills, in the Universities and Polytechnics in Leeds and Bradford. Young workers joining the industry receive careful training and many attend courses at the Colleges and Universities. Even experienced workers must learn about new methods which are being introduced in the mills.

The Growth of the Wool Textile Industry in West Yorkshire

In the eighteenth century cloth making in West Yorkshire was not carried out in large factory towns but in stone cottages high in the Pennines. Most of the raw wool was obtained from sheep

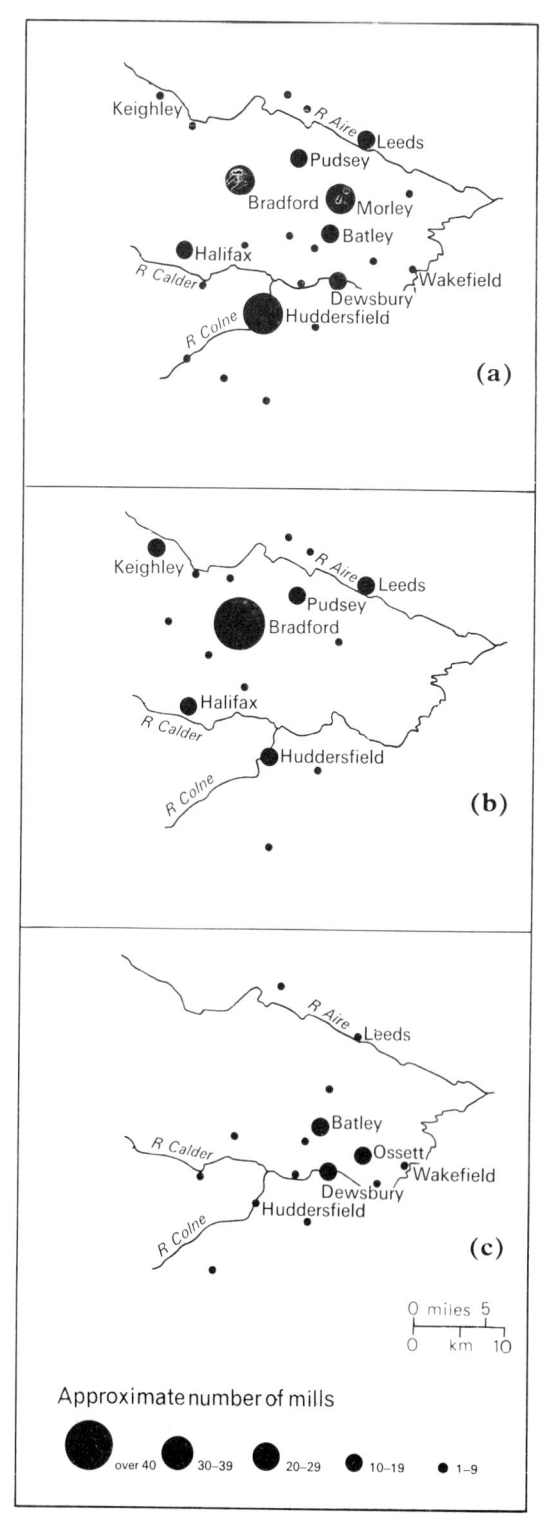

84 *The distribution of (a) woollen; (b) worsted and (c) mungo and shoddy mills in West Yorkshire*

eared locally. All the family was kept busy working either outside on the farm or indoors making cloth. At first only simple machines which could be worked by hand were used. The women and children carded the wool using wire brushes and made it up into yarn with spinning wheels; upstairs, the men wove the cloth on simple looms.

The cloth was washed and shrunk at the village fulling mill sited by the side of the stream. The soft-water streams which flow off the Millstone Grit moors were an advantage in washing greasy wool. Nowadays water can be softened artificially and detergents make it easier to clean the fleeces.

After fulling the cloth was stretched out to dry on a 'tenter'—a wooden frame which stood out in the fields near the weaver's cottage. The cloth was then taken down the valleys by packhorse for sale at the cloth markets in places like Halifax.

Great changes occurred in the eighteenth century which altered the whole landscape of West Yorkshire. Over the Pennines in Lancashire new machines were invented for making cotton cloth. The most important of these, Kay's flying shuttle, Hargreaves' spinning jenny and Arkwright's carding machine, were quickly adapted in West Yorkshire for making wool cloth. At first, men who were afraid of losing their jobs resisted the introduction of these new machines. They were called 'Luddites' and attacked the mills and smashed machinery. Wool guilds in York and other parts of Yorkshire, in East Anglia and the West Country, were also opposed to the new machines. Soon the markets were flooded with cheap machine-made cloth from West Yorkshire. As a result the woollen industry declined in other areas but prospered in West Yorkshire.

At first the new machines were driven by water wheels and mills were sited along the banks of small Pennine streams. Later steam engines were invented which drove machinery more efficiently and could be fired with coal mined nearby in the Yorkshire Coalfield. Large new mills were built further down the valleys in small towns on or near the coalfield. People no longer found it profitable to make cloth in their own homes and many left their cottages high in the Pennines to live in rows of houses built for workers near the new mills. In this way the manufacture of cloth changed from a domestic to a factory industry. The migration of workers from the countryside caused the rapid growth of towns in West Yorkshire.

So much cloth was produced that raw wool had to be imported from abroad. This led to the cutting of canals and later to the building of railways and the improvement of roads, along the Pennine valleys like the Calder. By these means, wool towns like Halifax were connected with the coalfield and with the ports of Hull and Liverpool for the importing of raw materials and food and for the exporting of cloth.

The Clothing Industry

The clothing factories of Leeds are the largest market for cloths made in West Yorkshire. Here at Hudson Road Mills is the chief factory and head office of Burton Tailoring Ltd, one of the world's largest tailoring organisations.

The firm takes its name from the late Sir Montague Burton who in 1901 opened a one-man tailoring shop in Chesterfield with £100 borrowed from a relative. He worked a seventeen-hour day making suits which he then sold from door to door. Now, the company he founded owns the biggest chain of men's wear shops in Britain and has branches in other European countries.

Not all the clothes manufactured by Burton's are made in Leeds because the Company has other factories elsewhere in Yorkshire and Lancashire. Wherever they are made, the suits need many manufacturing operations.

First of all they are cut out by hand from lengths of cloth by cutters like the one seen in the photograph (Fig 85). He has a very skilled job. Boys leaving school who wish to become cutters must serve an apprenticeship and attend classes at a technical college. Behind the cutter is a rack of templates which he uses as a guide for marking out the cloth. He does not rely on these entirely, but adjusts each pattern according to the customer's measurements and the style he requires. He gets this information from the form in front of him which was completed when the order was placed in the shop. His only other equipment is a long bench on which he can spread out the cloth, a tape measure, a yardstick, a piece of tailor's chalk and a pair of shears.

The sewing is done by separate coat and trouser departments where the pieces of cloth are carried by conveyors to workers who com-

85 *A cutter at work in the Montague Burton clothing factory, Leeds*

plete operations such as button holing, sleeving and pocket making. Machines are used whereever possible, but some hand stitching still has to be done. Many of the workers here have passed through the training department: usually about seventy school leavers a year are selected for training at the Leeds factory. After tailoring the suits have to be pressed and checked carefully for any defects before being sent to the branch shops in the firm's own vans.

Leeds is the home of many other tailoring organisations including Jacksons which merged with Burtons in 1952. A few other clothing firms with factories in Leeds are Barrans, John Collier, Alexandre, Benjamin Simon, Hepworths, and Sumrie. The oldest of them is Barrans whose founder, John Barran, was the first to adopt the sewing machine invented in America by Singer. He laid the foundation of the clothing industry in Leeds which today employs 30,000 people. Not all of them work in large factories like Hudson Road Mills; there are still many small workshops.

Like many other industries in Britain the clothing industry now suffers from competition from cheaper goods imported from places like Hong Kong where wages and other production costs are lower than they are here. The clothing industry has also suffered from a fall in demand as casual clothes have become more fashionable. As a result some clothing factories are being closed and others reduced in size.

The Engineering Industry

Over 750 years ago the monks built an ironworks on the floor of the Aire valley close to their abbey at Kirkstall, Leeds. Now only the ruins of the abbey remain, but on the site of the forge stands the works of Kirkstall Forge Engineering Ltd, where axles for motor vehicles are made.

Today the engineering industry of Leeds

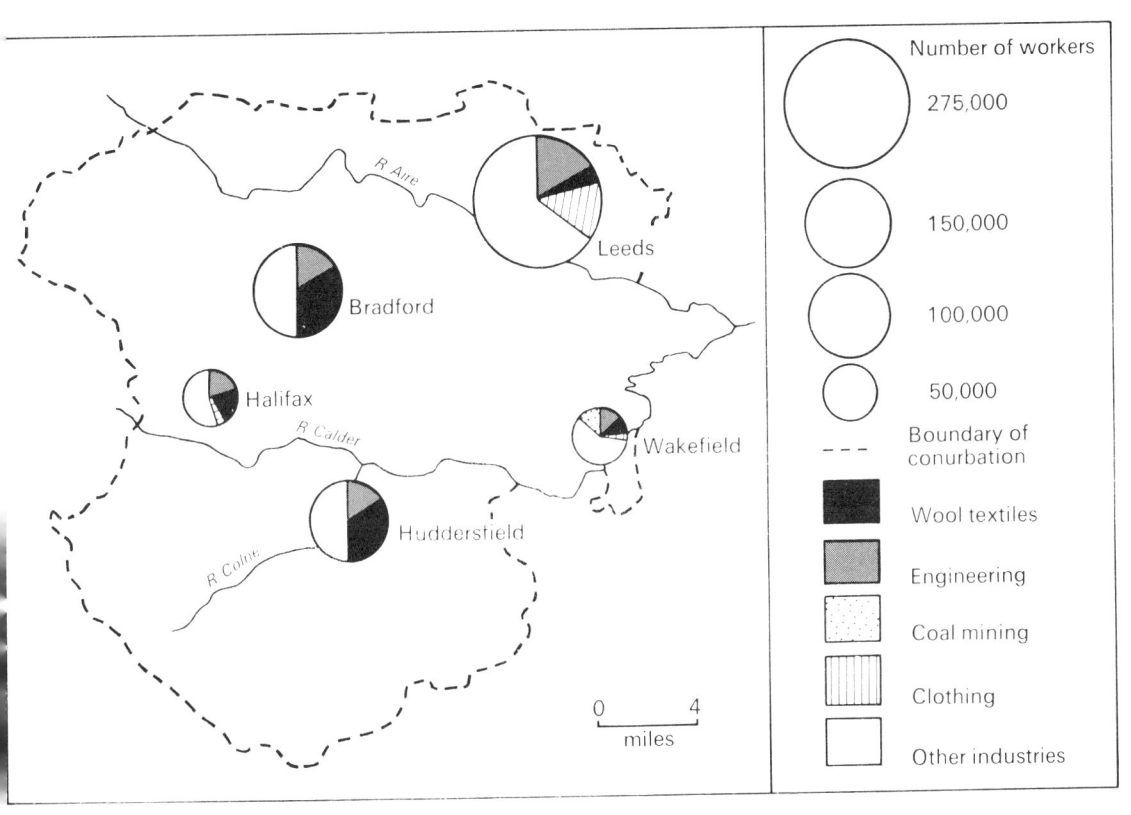

86 *Employment in the larger towns of West Yorkshire (1971 figures)*

employs forty-five thousand people. A short list of Leeds firms and their products is given below. It shows that they manufacture a wide range of goods.

Hunslet Engine Co
    Diesel locomotives
Monk Bridge Iron and Steel Co
    Jet engine parts
West Yorkshire Foundries Ltd
    Motor car parts
British Screw Co
    Nuts, bolts and screws
Thomas Smith and Sons Ltd
    Cranes and excavators
Thomas Green and Sons Ltd
    Agricultural and gardening equipment
Greenwood and Batley Ltd
    Steam turbines and machine tools
Catton and Co Ltd
    Magnetic, stainless and heat resistant steels.

Most of the works are found on the floor of the Aire valley. The map (Fig. 86) shows that engineering is important throughout West Yorkshire. Many of the works developed during the Industrial Revolution to supply machinery to the growing mining and textile industries. Even today, mining machinery is made in Wakefield and textile machinery at Bradford and Keighley.

When the industry was first developed, coal from the Yorkshire Coalfield was used to smelt iron ores obtained from thin bands in the coal measures. Now there are no blast furnaces in the area because iron and steel can be made more cheaply in other areas such as Sheffield, Rotherham, Scunthorpe and Teesside.

The Centre of Leeds
Functional Zones. The photograph (Fig 87) of the centre of Leeds shows the Headrow on the right and Briggate on the left. Notice that most of the buildings are shops and that some of them, e.g. Burton and Etam, belong to firms which have branches in towns all over Britain.

On the corner opposite Burton's at the junction

of Briggate and The Headrow is Lewis's department store. It is not shown on the photograph, but its position can be seen from the street plan (Fig 88). 120,000 people shopped at the store on the day it was opened in 1932. It has five floors and over 150 departments each selling a particular line of goods. Only in large cities like Leeds, which can attract thousands of regular shoppers, is it profitable to build stores as big as this. Woolworths, Marks and Spencer, Littlewoods and Debenhams all have stores in the main shopping centre. There are also many smaller shops which specialise in the sale of clothing, furniture, footwear and jewellery.

Marked on the street plan is Kirkgate Market, which has been partially rebuilt after a major fire in 1975. On a busy Saturday more than 100,000 people shop there, especially for fruit, vegetables, fish, meat and poultry. The market stands on the edge of the main shopping centre which is bounded by Vicar Lane, Albion Street, The Headrow and Boar Lane.

Many business organisations such as banks, building societies and insurance companies have their offices in the area between City Square, The Headrow, Albion Street and East Parade.

New multi-storey office blocks are a feature of this part of Leeds.

Notice that most of the important public buildings including the Town Hall and the University stand to the north of The Headrow and south-west of Woodhouse Lane. Many of the cinemas and restaurants are found in the area between New Briggate and Vicar Lane. The Grand Theatre is also found in this part of the city. After Christmas many people combine a day's shopping at the January sales with a visit to the pantomime at the Grand. Along Regent Street there are motor car showrooms, garages, firms selling car accessories and the R.A.C. office.

This concentration of similar services into zones is typical of the centres of large towns all over Britain.

Traffic. In the photograph (Fig 87), all the vehicles in Briggate are facing in the same direction, because of the one-way-street system which was introduced in the centre of Leeds, as in other town centres, to relieve traffic congestion. Most of the important shopping streets in the area bounded by Park Row, The Headrow, Vicar Lane and Boar Lane have been converted to pedestrian

87 *The centre of Leeds, showing Briggate and the Headrow*

precincts, creating the largest such precinct in Europe.

Traffic congestion is worst on Saturdays, when the town is full of shoppers, and on weekdays during the morning and evening 'rush hours' when people are travelling to and from work. The majority of people in Leeds live in the suburbs but most of the shops, offices and factories are concentrated in the city centre. Consequently people have to travel into the town to work and shop. The traffic congestion is made worse by people who drive into Leeds by car from nearby 'dormitory' towns.

Schemes like the Merrion Centre help to ease the traffic problem. This pedestrian area has shops, supermarkets, restaurants, offices, banks, a cinema, and a petrol station. There is also a multi-storey car park where people can leave their cars.

At Seacroft, just inside the city boundary on the outer ring road, Leeds has built a 'satellite' town. This has its own shopping centre and work is provided for the residents by a new industrial estate. Soon it will have enough homes for 80,000 people. Many families have already been rehoused there from slum-clearance areas in the older parts of the city.

The new inner ring road, shown on the street plan, is an urban motorway which has helped to solve the traffic problem. Traffic can now drive round instead of through the city centre.

Communications. People travelling into Leeds by public transport arrive either by rail at City Station or by bus at one of the bus stations marked on the street plan. The Passenger Transport Executive runs services to and from all parts of the city from the Central Bus Station near Kirkgate Market. Long distance services are now operated by the West Yorkshire Passenger Transport Executive and the National Bus Company.

An atlas map of Britain will show that Leeds

88 *A street plan of central Leeds*

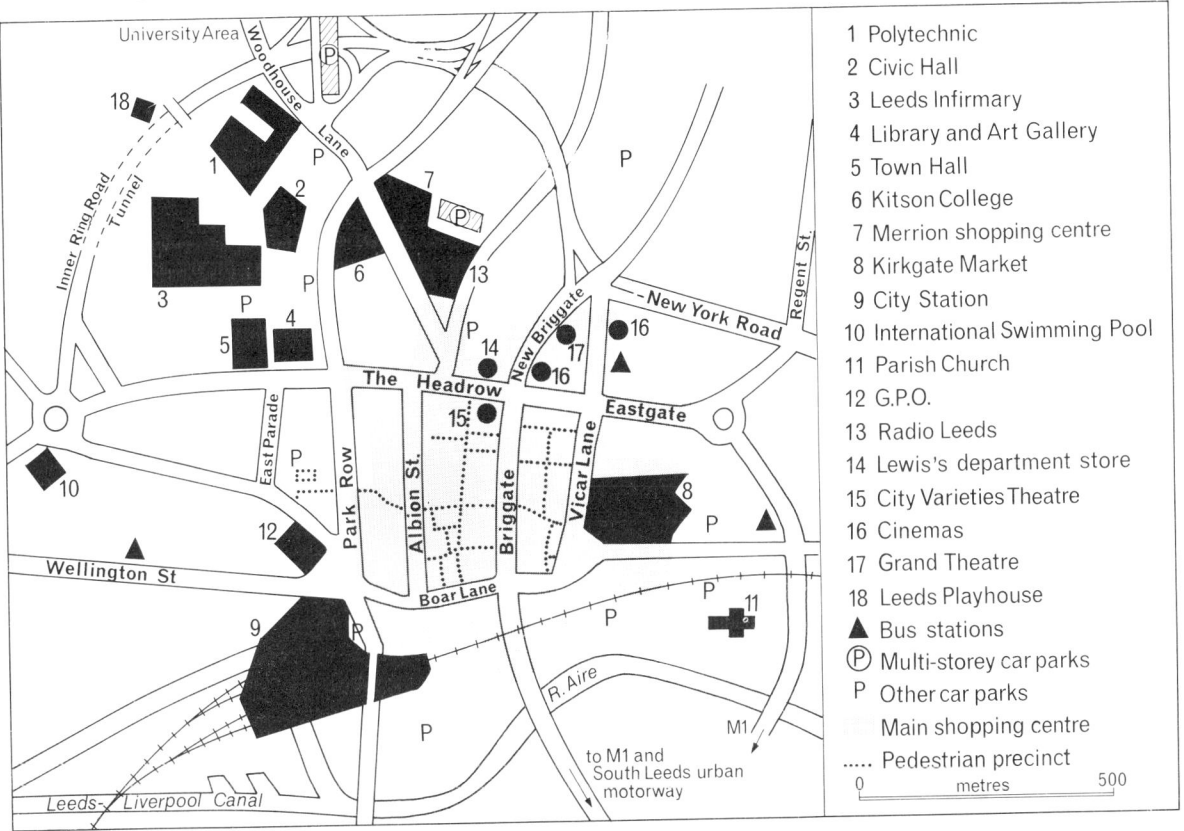

stands at the crossing point of many railway lines. Among these are the trans-Pennine route between Liverpool and Hull and the lines between London and Scotland via Newcastle and Carlisle. A new liner train terminal has been opened at Stourton alongside the northern end of the M1 motorway.

Despite its inland position, Leeds is linked with the North Sea by the Aire and Calder Navigation and through the Aire Gap to the Irish Sea by the Leeds–Liverpool Canal. Both of these are marked on the street plan. Warehouses and factories are situated alongside these waterways on the floor of the Aire valley. A new terminal has been built at Hunslet by British Waterways. Here barges unload cargoes of fuel oil which have been brought from Hull.

The Conurbation
The map (Fig 89) shows that the Ordnance Survey extract (Map D) covers only a small part of a much larger area where closely spaced towns and villages merge into each other. Such a continuous built up area is called a 'conurbation' and much of the metropolitan county of West Yorkshire can be so described. Notice from the map how the urban areas centred around the middle Aire and Calder valleys give way to various types of more rural land to the north, south, east, and west.

The conurbation is the biggest industrial area in the Yorkshire and North Lincolnshire region. It provides jobs for many thousands of people who either live there or travel daily from surrounding 'dormitory' settlements or outlying villages. The map (Fig. 86) shows that Leeds, marked with the largest circle, has most workers. The other towns employ fewer people and have smaller circles on the map. Each circle has been divided up according to the number of workers in different industries. Notice how wool textiles is the largest industry, especially in Bradford, Halifax, and Huddersfield. Next comes engineering which has more workers than textiles in

89 *West Yorkshire Metropolitan County, showing the conurbation, main roads and motorways*

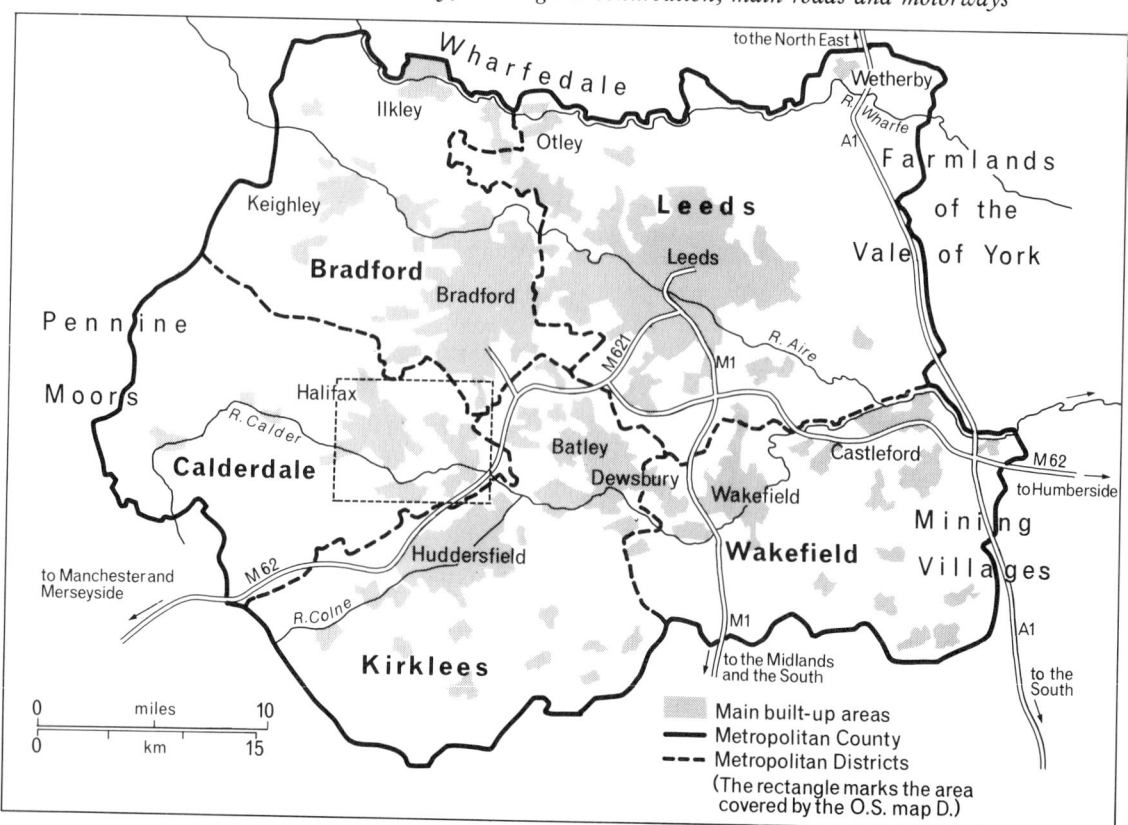

Leeds. Mining has most workers east of Wakefield while the clothing industry is concentrated in Leeds. The other industries include services such as shops, banks, offices and entertainments. Local government employs many office workers in Wakefield which was the capital of the old West Riding and is the administrative centre for the new West Yorkshire Metropolitan County. Leeds, as the major city of the region, has many government and commercial offices.

Over 2 million people live in West Yorkshire, most of them in the large towns and cities. The county is now divided into five metropolitan districts: Leeds (744,500), Bradford (458,900), Kirklees (372,500), Wakefield (306,500) and Calderdale (190,100). The map (Fig 90) shows that this is the largest area in the Yorkshire and North Lincolnshire region with a high density of population. Similar but smaller areas of dense population occur in South Yorkshire along the Don Valley, in Cleveland around the Tees estuary, and in Humberside at towns like Hull, Grimsby,

90 *The distribution of population in the Yorkshire and North Lincolnshire Region*

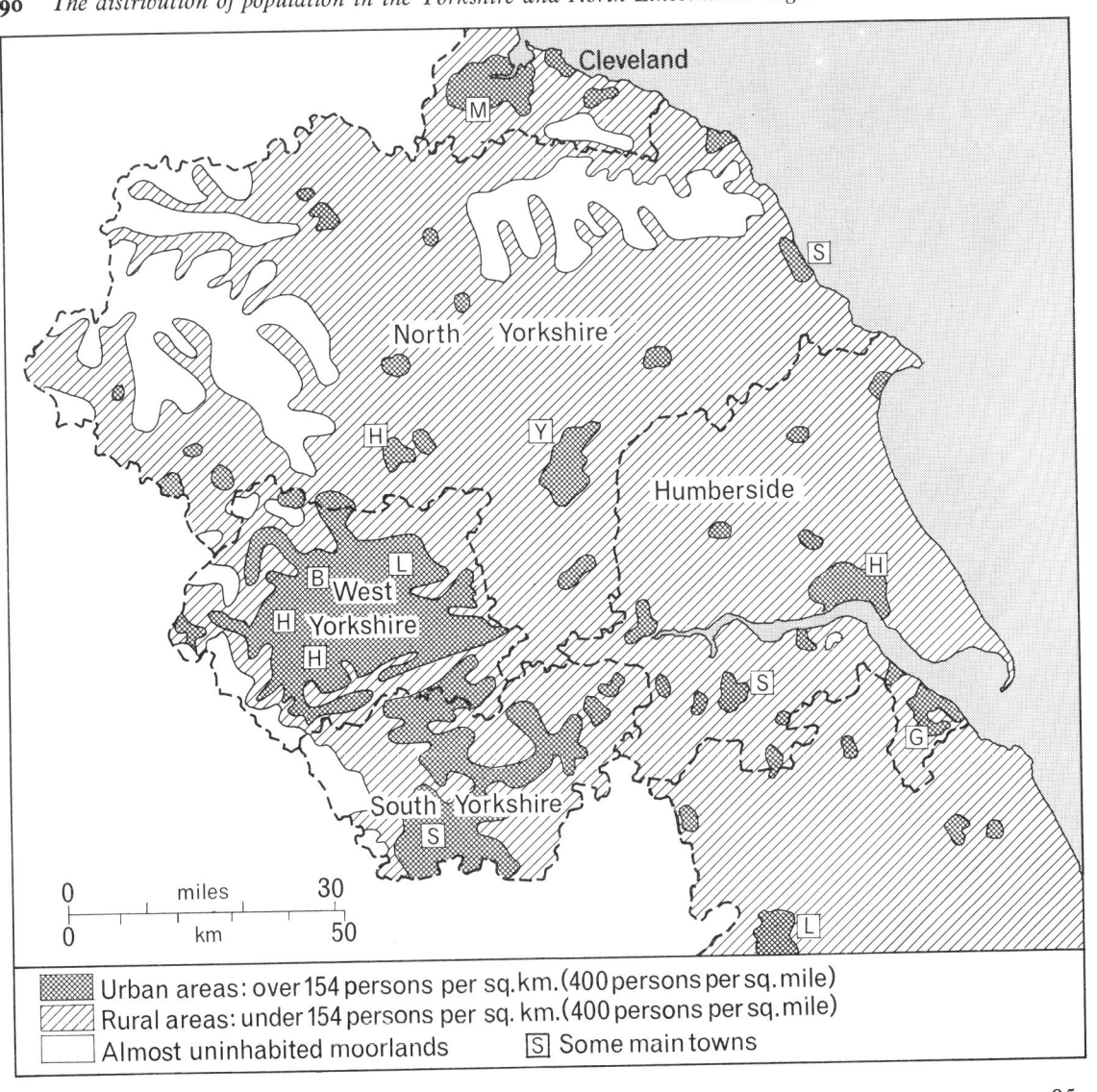

and Scunthorpe. These densely peopled areas contrast with the more lightly populated county of North Yorkshire. Apart from the large towns of York, Harrogate and Scarborough, this county includes the almost uninhabited higher parts of the Pennines and North York Moors as well as large stretches of countryside with scattered market towns and villages.

Work to do

1. Study Fig 78 in Chapter 9 and then make a similar sketch of Fig 81. On it mark and name: the railway and railway station; the power station; a church with a tower; a church with a steeple; a modern factory; an older factory; an area of terrace houses; a modern housing estate; two areas of tower blocks.
2. Using the Ordnance Survey map (Map D), draw a sketch cross section of the Calder valley from the grid reference 125200 to the triangulation station at 108236. On it mark and name: Elland Park Wood; the Calder; the canal; the railway; the A6025; Elland Upper Edge; the quarry at 123206; the works at 119220; the triangulation point. Put a title and approximate vertical and horizontal scales.
3. In the school library, find out about scouring, carding, combing, dyeing and cloth finishing. Then write an essay on 'How wool cloths are made in the mills of West Yorkshire.'
4. Using classified telephone directories and a map of postal districts, make distribution maps for the main industries in your local area.
5. Why did West Yorkshire become the centre of the wool textile industry?
6. Using the street plan (Fig 88) as a guide, make a map to show the centre of Leeds divided up into: the shopping centre; the business district; the entertainment area; the motor trades area; the civic area (where most of the public buildings are found). Add the bus stations, the canals, the River Aire, the railways and City Station. Make a similar map of your local town.
7. Make a shopping survey in the main street in your local town. Make a map to show the position of the different kinds of shops you have found there.
8. Carry out a shopping survey at: (a) a street corner shop; (b) a suburban shopping centre; (c) the centre of the local town. Estimate the number of shoppers a day at a shop in each of these places. Try to make a map to show where the shoppers come from to shop at each of these places and to account for the differences.
9. Make maps of your local town to show: (a) the one-way street system; (b) streets with no parking, parking meters and time limits on parking; (c) car parks; (d) multistorey car parks; (e) ring roads and bypasses; (f) pedestrian precincts. Suggest ways in which traffic congestion could be reduced.
10. Study a recent R.A.C. or A.A. book and then make a map of Yorkshire and North Lincolnshire to show: (a) the main towns; (b) the main roads; (c) the existing and proposed motorways.
11. Find out from your local council officers or information office the name of the county and district in which you live. What responsibilities do the county council and the district council have? How are councillors elected?
12. Study the population statistics shown on Page 2 of this book. Attempt to explain changes which are expected to have occurred by 1991.